Healthy Eating

STAR
FIRE

This is a Starfire book
First published in 2004

04 06 07 05

3 5 7 9 10 8 6 4 2

Starfire is part of
The Foundry Creative Media Company Limited
Crabtree Hall, Crabtree Lane, Fulham, London, SW6 6TY

Visit the Foundry website: www.foundry.co.uk/recipes

ISBN: 1-844512-07-X

The CIP record for this book is available from the British Library.

Printed in China

ACKNOWLEDGEMENTS

Authors: Catherine Atkinson, Juliet Barker, Liz Martin, Vicki Smallwood, Gina Steer,
Carol Tennant, Mari Mererid Williams, Elizabeth Wolf-Cohen and Simone Wright
Editorial Consultant: Gina Steer
Project Editors: Karen Fitzpatrick and Sarah Goulding
Photography: Colin Bowling, Paul Forrester and Stephen Brayne
Home Economists and Stylists: Jacqueline Bellefontaine,
Mandy Phipps, Vicki Smallwood and Penny Stephens
Design Team: Helen Courtney, Jennifer Bishop, Lucy Bradbury and Chris Herbert

All props supplied by Barbara Stewart at Surfaces

NOTE
Recipes using uncooked eggs should be avoided by infants,
the elderly, pregnant women and anyone suffering from an illness.

CONTENTS

SOUPS & STARTERS

FISH

MEAT

POULTRY

VEGETABLES & SALADS

ENTERTAINING

HYGIENE IN THE KITCHEN

I t is well worth remembering that many foods can carry some form of bacteria. In most cases, the worst it will lead to is a bout of food poisoning or gastroenteritis, but for certain groups this can be more serious and the risk can be reduced or eliminated by good food hygiene and proper cooking.

Do not buy food that is past its sell-by date and do not consume any food that is past its use-by date. When buying food, use the eyes and nose. If the food looks tired, limp or a bad colour or it has a rank, acrid or simply bad smell, do not buy or eat it under any circumstances.

Do take special care when preparing raw meat and fish. A separate chopping board should be used for each; wash the knife, board and the hands thoroughly before handling or preparing any other food.

Regularly clean, defrost and clear out the refrigerator or freezer – it is worth checking the packaging to see exactly how long each product is safe to freeze.

Avoid handling food if suffering from an upset stomach as bacteria can be passed through food preparation.

Dish cloths and tea towels must be washed and changed regularly. Ideally use disposable cloths which should be replaced on a daily basis. More durable cloths should be left to soak in bleach, then washed in the washing machine on a boil wash.

Keep the hands, cooking utensils and food preparation surfaces clean and do not allow pets to climb on to any work surfaces.

BUYING

A void bulk buying where possible, especially fresh produce such as meat, poultry, fish, fruit and vegetables. Fresh foods lose their nutritional value rapidly so buying a little at a time minimises loss of nutrients. It also eliminates a packed refrigerator which reduces the effectiveness of the refrigeration process.

When buying prepackaged goods such as cans or pots of cream and yogurts, check that the packaging is intact and not damaged or pierced at all. Cans should not be dented, pierced or rusty. Check the sell-by dates even

for cans and packets of dry ingredients such as flour and rice. Store fresh foods in the refrigerator as soon as possible – not in the car or the office.

When buying frozen foods, ensure that they are not heavily iced on the outside and the contents feel completely frozen. Ensure that the frozen foods have been stored in the cabinet at the correct storage level and the temperature is below -18°C/-64°F. Pack in cool bags to transport home and place in the freezer as soon as possible after purchase.

PREPARATION

M ake sure that all work surfaces and utensils are clean and dry. Hygiene should be given priority at all times.

Separate chopping boards should be used for raw and cooked meats, fish and vegetables. Currently, a variety of good-quality plastic boards come in various designs and colours. This makes differentiating easier and the plastic has the added hygienic advantage of being washable at high temperatures in the dishwasher. If using the board for fish, first wash in cold water, then in hot to prevent odour. Also, remember that knives and utensils should always be thoroughly cleaned after use.

When cooking, be particularly careful to keep cooked and raw food separate to avoid any contamination. It is worth washing all fruits and vegetables regardless of whether they are going to be eaten raw or lightly cooked. This rule should apply even to prewashed herbs and salads.

Do not reheat food more than once. If using a microwave, always check that the food is piping hot all the way through. (In theory, the food should reach 70°C/158°F and needs to be cooked at that temperature for at least three minutes to ensure that all bacteria are killed.)

All poultry must be thoroughly thawed before using, including chicken and poussin. Remove the food to be thawed from the freezer and place in a shallow dish to contain the juices. Leave the food in the refrigerator until it is completely thawed. A 1.4 kg/3 lb whole chicken will take about 26–30 hours to thaw. To speed up the process immerse the chicken in cold water. However, make sure that the water is changed regularly. When the joints can move freely and no ice crystals remain in the cavity, the bird is completely thawed.

Once thawed, remove the wrapper and pat the chicken dry. Place the chicken in a shallow dish, cover lightly and store as close to the base of the refrigerator as possible. The chicken should be cooked as soon as possible.

Some foods can be cooked from frozen including many prepacked foods such as soups, sauces, casseroles and breads. Where applicable follow the manufacturers' instructions.

Vegetables and fruits can also be cooked from frozen, but meats and fish should be thawed first. The only time food can be refrozen is when the food has been thoroughly thawed then cooked. Once the food has cooled then it can be frozen again. On such occasions the food can only be stored for one month.

All poultry and game (except for duck) must be cooked thoroughly. When cooked the juices will run clear on the thickest part of the bird – the best area to try is usually the thigh. Other meats, like minced meat and pork should be cooked right the way through. Fish should turn opaque, be firm in texture and break easily into large flakes.

When cooking leftovers, make sure they are reheated until piping hot and that any sauce or soup reaches boiling point first.

STORING
REFRIGERATING AND FREEZING

Meat, poultry, fish, seafood and dairy products should all be refrigerated. The temperature of the refrigerator should be between 1–5°C/34–41°F while the freezer temperature should not rise above -18°C/-0.4°F.

To ensure the optimum refrigerator and freezer temperature, avoid leaving the door open for long periods of time. Try not to overstock the refrigerator as this reduces the airflow inside and prevents effective refrigeration.

When refrigerating cooked food, allow it to cool down quickly and completely before refrigerating. Hot food will raise the temperature of the refrigerator and possibly affect or spoil other food stored in it.

Food within the refrigerator and freezer should always be covered. Raw and cooked food should be stored in separate parts of the refrigerator. Cooked food should be kept on the top shelves of the refrigerator, while raw meat, poultry and fish should be placed on bottom shelves to avoid drips and cross-contamination. It is recommended that eggs should be refrigerated in order to maintain their freshness and shelf life.

Take care that frozen foods are not stored in the freezer for too long. Blanched vegetables can be stored for one month; beef, lamb, poultry and pork for six months and unblanched vegetables and fruits in syrup for a year. Oily fish and sausages should be stored for three months. Dairy products can last four to six months while cakes and pastries should be kept in the freezer for three to six months.

HIGH-RISK FOODS

Certain foods may carry risks to people who are considered vulnerable such as the elderly, the ill, pregnant women, babies, young infants and those suffering from a recurring illness.

It is advisable to avoid those foods listed below which belong to a higher-risk category.

There is a slight chance that some eggs carry the bacteria salmonella. Cook the eggs until both the yolk and the white are firm to eliminate this risk. Pay particular attention to dishes and products incorporating lightly-cooked or raw eggs which should be cut out of the diet. Sauces including Hollandaise, mayonnaise, mousses, soufflés and meringues all use raw or lightly-cooked eggs, as do custard-based dishes, ice creams and sorbets. These are all considered high-risk foods to the vulnerable groups mentioned above.

Certain meats and poultry also carry the potential risk of salmonella and so should be cooked thoroughly until the juices run clear and there is no pinkness left. Unpasteurised products such as milk, cheese (especially soft cheese), pâté and meat (both raw and cooked) all have the potential risk of listeria and should be avoided.

When buying seafood, buy from a reputable source which has a high turnover to ensure freshness. Fish should have bright clear eyes, shiny skin and bright pink or red gills. The fish should feel stiff to the touch, with a slight smell of sea air and iodine. The flesh of fish steaks and fillets should be translucent with no signs of discolouration. Molluscs such as scallops, clams and mussels are sold fresh and are still alive. Avoid any that are open or do not close when tapped lightly. In the same way, univalves such as cockles or winkles should withdraw back into their shells when lightly prodded. When choosing cephalopods such as squid and octopus they should have a firm flesh and pleasant sea smell.

As with all fish, whether it is shellfish or seafish, care is required when freezing. It is imperative to check whether the fish has been frozen before. If it has been, then it should not be frozen again under any circumstances.

NUTRITION
The Role of Essential Nutrients

A healthy and well-balanced diet is the body's primary energy source. In children, it constitutes the building blocks for future health as well as providing lots of energy. In adults, it encourages self-healing and regeneration within the body. A well-balanced diet will provide the body with all the essential nutrients it needs. This can be achieved by eating a variety of foods, demonstrated in the pyramid below.

FATS

PROTEINS

milk,	meat, fish,
yogurt	poultry, eggs,
and cheese	nuts and pulses

FRUITS AND VEGETABLES

STARCHY CARBOHYDRATES
cereals, potatoes, bread, rice and pasta

FATS

Fats fall into two categories: saturated and unsaturated. It is very important that a healthy balance is achieved within the diet. Fats are an essential part of the diet, a source of energy and provide essential fatty acids and fat soluble vitamins. The right balance of fats should boost the body's immunity to infection and keep muscles, nerves and arteries in good condition. Saturated fats are of animal origin and are hard when stored at room temperature. They can be found in dairy produce, meat, eggs, margarines and hard white cooking fat (lard) as well as in manufactured products such as pies, biscuits and cakes. A high intake of saturated fat over many years has been proven to increase heart disease and high blood cholesterol levels and often leads to weight gain. The aim of a healthy diet is to keep the fat content low in the foods that we eat. Lowering the amount of saturated fat that we consume is very important, but this does not mean that it is good to consume lots of other types of fat.

There are two kinds of unsaturated fats: polyunsaturated fats and monounsaturated fats. Polyunsaturated fats include the following oils: safflower, soybean, corn and sesame. Within the polyunsaturated group are Omega oils. The Omega-3 oils are of significant interest because they have been found to be particularly beneficial to coronary health and can encourage brain growth and development. Omega-3 oils are derived from oily fish such as salmon, mackerel, herring, pilchards and sardines. It is recommended that we should eat these types of fish at least once a week. However, for those who do not eat fish or who are vegetarians, liver oil supplements are available in most supermarkets and health shops. It is suggested that these supplements should be taken on a daily basis. The most popular oils that are high in monounsaturates are olive oil, sunflower oil and peanut oil. The Mediterranean diet which is based on a diet high in monounsaturated fats is recommended for heart health. Also, monounsaturated fats are known to help reduce the levels of cholesterol.

PROTEINS

Composed of amino acids, proteins perform a wide variety of essential functions for the body including supplying energy and building and repairing tissues. Good sources of proteins are eggs, milk, yogurt, cheese, meat, fish, poultry, eggs, nuts and pulses. (See the second level of the pyramid.) Some of these foods, however, contain saturated fats. To strike a nutritional balance eat generous amounts of vegetable protein foods such as soya, beans, lentils, peas and nuts.

FRUITS AND VEGETABLES

Not only are fruits and vegetables the most visually appealing foods, but they are extremely good for us, providing essential vitamins and minerals needed for growth, repair and protection in the human body. Fruits and vegetables are low in calories and are responsible for regulating the body's metabolic processes and controlling the composition of its fluids and cells.

MINERALS

CALCIUM Important for healthy bones and teeth, nerve transmission, muscle contraction, blood clotting and hormone function. Calcium promotes a healthy heart, improves skin, relieves aching muscles and bones, maintains the correct acid-alkaline balance and reduces menstrual cramps. Good sources are dairy products, small bones of small fish, nuts, pulses, fortified white flours, breads and green leafy vegetables.

CHROMIUM Part of the glucose tolerance factor, chromium balances blood sugar levels, helps to normalise hunger and reduce cravings, improves lifespan, helps protect DNA and is essential for heart function. Good sources are brewer's yeast, wholemeal bread, rye bread, oysters, potatoes, green peppers, butter and parsnips.

IODINE Important for the manufacture of thyroid hormones and for normal development. Good sources of iodine are seafood, seaweed, milk and dairy products.

IRON As a component of haemoglobin, iron carries oxygen around the body. It is vital for normal growth and development. Good sources are liver, corned beef, red meat, fortified breakfast cereals, pulses, green leafy vegetables, egg yolk, cocoa and cocoa products.

MAGNESIUM Important for efficient functioning of metabolic enzymes and development of the skeleton. Magnesium promotes healthy muscles by helping them to relax and is therefore good for PMS. It is also important for heart muscles and the nervous system. Good sources are nuts, green vegetables, meat, cereals, milk and yogurt.

PHOSPHORUS Forms and maintains bones and teeth, builds muscle tissue, helps maintain the pH of the body and aids metabolism and energy production. Phosphorus is present in almost all foods.

POTASSIUM Enables nutrients to move into cells, while waste products move out; promotes healthy nerves and muscles; maintains fluid balance in the body; helps secretion of insulin for blood sugar control to produce constant energy; relaxes muscles; maintains heart functioning; and stimulates gut movement to encourage proper elimination. Good sources are fruit, vegetables, milk and bread.

SELENIUM Antioxidant properties help to protect against free radicals and carcinogens. Selenium reduces inflammation, stimulates the immune system to fight infections, promotes a healthy heart and helps vitamin E's action. It is also required for the male reproductive system and is needed for metabolism. Good sources are tuna, liver, kidney, meat, eggs, cereals, nuts and dairy products.

SODIUM Important in helping to control body fluid and balance, preventing dehydration. Sodium is involved in muscle and nerve function and helps move nutrients into cells. All foods are good sources, however processed, pickled and salted foods are richest in sodium and should be eaten in moderation.

ZINC Important for metabolism and the healing of wounds. It also aids ability to cope with stress, promotes a healthy nervous system and brain especially in the growing foetus, aids bones and teeth formation and is essential for constant energy. Good sources are liver, meat, pulses, whole-grain cereals, nuts and oysters.

VITAMINS

VITAMIN A Important for cell growth and developmemt and for the formation of visual pigments in the eye. Vitamin A comes in two forms: retinol and beta-carotenes. Retinol is found in liver, meat and meat products and whole milk and its products. Beta-carotene is a powerful antioxidant and is found in red and yellow fruits and vegetables such as carrots, mangoes and apricots.

VITAMIN B1 Important in releasing energy from carbohydrate-containing foods. Good sources are yeast and yeast products, bread, fortified breakfast cereals and potatoes.

VITAMIN B2 Important for metabolism of proteins, fats and carbohydrates to produce energy. Good sources are meat, yeast extracts, fortified breakfast cereals and milk and its products.

VITAMIN B3 Required for the metabolism of food into energy production. Good sources are milk and milk products, fortified breakfast cereals, pulses, meat, poultry and eggs.

VITAMIN B5 Important for the metabolism of food and energy production. All foods are good sources but especially fortified breakfast cereals, whole-grain bread and dairy products.

VITAMIN B6 Important for metabolism of protein and fat. Vitamin B6 may also be involved in the regulation of sex hormones. Good sources are liver, fish, pork, soya beans and peanuts.

VITAMIN B12 Important for the production of red blood cells and DNA. It is vital for growth and the nervous system. Good sources are meat, fish, eggs, poultry and milk.

BIOTIN Important for metabolism of fatty acids. Good sources of biotin are liver, kidney, eggs and nuts. Micro-organisms also manufacture this vitamin in the gut.

VITAMIN C Important for healing wounds and the formation of collagen which keeps skin and bones strong. It is an important antioxidant. Good sources are fruits, especially soft summer fruits, and vegetables.

VITAMIN D Important for absorption and handling of calcium to help build bone strength. Good sources are oily fish, eggs, whole milk and milk products, margarine and of course sufficient exposure to sunlight, as vitamin D is made in the skin.

VITAMIN E Important as an antioxidant vitamin helping to protect cell membranes from damage. Good sources are vegetable oils, margarine, seeds, nuts and green vegetables.

FOLIC ACID Critical during pregnancy for the development of the brain and nerves. It is always essential for brain and nerve function and is needed for utilising protein and red blood cell formation. Good sources are whole-grain cereals, fortified breakfast cereals, green leafy vegetables, oranges and liver.

VITAMIN K Important for controlling blood clotting. Good sources are cauliflower, Brussels sprouts, lettuce, cabbage, beans, broccoli, peas, asparagus, potatoes, corn oil, tomatoes and milk.

CARBOHYDRATES

Carbohydrates are an energy source and come in two forms: starch and sugar. Starch carbohydrates are also known as complex carbohydrates and they include all cereals, potatoes, breads, rice and pasta. (See the fourth level of the pyramid). Eating whole-grain varieties of these foods also provides fibre. Diets high in fibre are believed to be beneficial in helping to prevent bowel cancer and can also keep cholesterol down. High-fibre diets are also good for those concerned about weight gain. Fibre is bulky and fills the stomach, therefore reducing hunger pangs. Sugar carbohydrates are also known as fast-release carbohydrates (because of the quick fix of energy they give to the body) and include sugar and sugar-sweetened products such as jams and syrups. Milk provides lactose which is a milk sugar and fruits provide fructose which is a fruit sugar.

VARIETIES OF RICE AND STORAGE

M any of the recipes in this book involve rice, a product that is the staple food of many countries throughout the world. Every country and culture has its own repertoire of rice recipes, for example, India has the aromatic biryani, Spain has the saffron-scented paella and Italy has the creamy risotto. Rice is grown on marshy, flooded land where other cereals cannot thrive and because it is grown in so many different areas, there is a huge range of rice types.

LONG-GRAIN WHITE RICE This is probably the most widely used type of rice. Long-grain white rice has been milled so

that the husk, bran and germ is removed. If you buy it loose, it is sometimes whitened with chalk or other substances, so thorough rinsing under cold running water is essential. Easy-cook long-grain white rice has been steamed under pressure before milling. This makes it difficult to overcook, therefore separate dry and fluffy grains are virtually guaranteed. Precooked rice, also known as parboiled or converted rice, is polished white rice which is half cooked after milling, then dried again. It is quick and simple to cook, but has a rather bland flavour. Java rice is one of the slightly shorter long-grain rices and because it is particularly absorbent is often used in baked rice dishes.

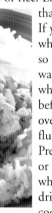

Rice is sometimes referred to by the country or region in which it was originally grown. Patna rice is a term used to describe a type of long-grain rice which originated from Patna in north-east India. Long-grain rice is rarely labelled by country of origin, as it now mostly comes from America. Carolina is simply another name for long-grain rice and refers to the region in America where rice was first planted.

LONG-GRAIN BROWN RICE Here the outer husk is removed leaving the bran and germ behind, so retaining a lot more of the fibre, vitamins and minerals. It has a nutty, slightly chewy texture and because it is less refined takes longer to cook than long-grain white rice.

BASMATI RICE This slender long-grain rice, which may be white or brown, is grown in the foothills of the Himalayas. After harvesting, it is allowed to mature for a year, giving it a unique aromatic

flavour, hence its name which means fragrant. It produces perfect, separate, white and fluffy grains that frequently feature in Indian cooking.

RISOTTO RICE Grown in the north of Italy, this is the only rice that is suitable for making Italian risotto. The grains are plump and stubby and have the ability to absorb large quantities of liquid without becoming too soft, cooking to a creamy texture with a slight bite. The starchiness of risotto rice makes it a good addition to soups where it acts as a thickener. It can also be made into moulded rice dishes such as timbales, as the grains hold together without being too sticky. There are two grades of risotto rice, superfino and fino. Arborio rice is the most widely sold variety of the former, but you may also find carnaroli, Roma and baldo in Italian food shops and delicatessens. Fino rice, such as vialone nano has a slightly shorter grain, but the flavour is still excellent.

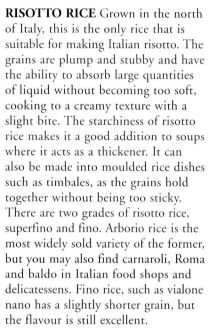

VALENCIA RICE Traditionally used for Spanish paella, Valencia rice is soft and tender when ready. The medium-sized grains break down easily, so should be left unstirred during cooking to absorb the flavour of the stock and other ingredients.

JASMINE RICE Also known as Thai fragrant rice, this long-grain rice has a delicate, almost perfumed aroma and flavour and a soft, sticky texture.

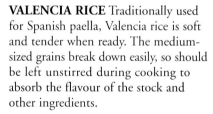

GLUTINOUS RICE White or black (unpolished), these short grains are high in starch and feature in Chinese and Japanese cooking, as the grains stick together when cooked making them easy to eat with chopsticks. This rice has a slightly sweet taste and is used for making dim sum as well as sweet, sticky puddings.

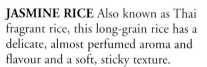

JAPANESE SUSHI RICE This is similar to glutinous rice in that it has a sticky texture. When mixed with rice vinegar it is easy to roll up with a filling inside to make sushi. Much of the sushi rice eaten in the West is now grown in California.

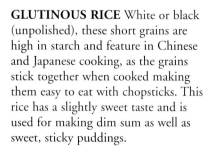

RICE PRODUCTS

N umerous Japanese ingredients are made from rice. Japan's national drink, sake, is a spirit distilled from rice and is often used in cooking. Mirin is a sweet rice wine used as a marinade in dishes such as teriyaki. Rice vinegar is made from soured and fermented wine. Japanese rice vinegar has a soft, mellow flavour, whereas Chinese rice vinegar has a very sharp taste.

Sometimes Japanese rice vinegars are made into flavoured vinegars by mixing the vinegar with soy sauce, for example, to make dashi. Most rice vinegars are a clear, pale golden colour, but brown rice vinegar, made from wholegrain rice, is deep brown.

Amasake is a rice drink, often sold in healthfood stores and is made by adding enzymes to wholegrain pudding rice. It can be used in puddings and baking as an alternative to milk.

Rice paper is made from a mixture of rice flour, salt and water. Machines roll the mixture out until it is extremely thin and transparent, then it is dried out. Rice paper comes in hard circles or triangles and is easily softened by placing between two dampened tea towels. When soft, the rice paper can be wrapped around a filling, then steamed or fried to make dishes such as pancake rolls or dim sum.

PUDDING RICE This rounded, short-grain rice is ideal for puddings and rice desserts. The grains swell and absorb large quantities of milk during cooking, giving puddings a rich and soft creamy consistency. Brown pudding rice is also available.

RED RICE This is grown in small amounts in the Camargue, a marshy region in Provence in France. It is similar to brown rice in taste and texture, but when cooked its red colour develops, making it an attractive addition to salads and other rice dishes.

WILD RICE Strictly speaking this is an aquatic grass which is grown in North America rather than a true variety of rice. Some wild rice is now grown commercially, which has reduced the price a little, but much of it is still found growing wild in North America's vast lakes, where only native Americans have the right to gather it. The black grains are long and slender and after harvesting and cleaning are toasted to remove the chaff and intensify the nutty flavour and slight chewiness. Although wild rice is much more expensive than other rices, a small quantity goes a long way – it is often sold as a mixture with either long-grain white or basmati rice.

FLAKED RICE White or brown rice grains are steamed and rolled to paper thinness to make flaked rice. It is extremely quick to cook and is mainly used to make creamy puddings, but may also be used for baking. It is sometimes found in commercially made muesli mixtures.

GROUND RICE This type of rice is made by grinding white rice to the texture of fine sand. Like flaked rice, it can be used to make fast rice puddings and is also frequently used in baking, especially for making biscuits such as shortbread.

RICE FLOUR Raw rice can be ground finely to make rice flour which may be used to thicken sauces (you need about 1 tablespoon to thicken 300 ml/½ pint of liquid) or as a vital ingredient in sticky Asian cakes and desserts. It is also used to make fresh and dried rice noodles. When rice flour is ground even more finely, it becomes rice powder and has a fine consistency like cornflour. It can be found in Asian food stores.

BUYING AND STORING RICE

R ice will keep for several years if kept in sealed packets, but it is at its best when fresh. To ensure freshness, always buy rice from reputable shops with a good turnover and buy in small quantities. Once opened, store the rice in an airtight container in a cool, dry place to keep out moisture. Most rices (but not risotto) benefit from washing before cooking – tip into a sieve and rinse under cold running water for a minute or so until the water runs clear.

Cooked rice will keep well for up to two days if cooled rapidly and stored in a bowl covered with clingfilm in the refrigerator. If eating rice cold, serve within 24 hours – after this time it should be reheated thoroughly. To reheat rice, place it in a heavy-based saucepan with 2–3 tablespoons of water, cover and heat until piping hot, shaking the pan occasionally. Alternatively, reheat the bowl of cooled rice in the microwave, piercing the clingfilm first.

COOKING TECHNIQUES FOR RICE

There are countless ways to cook rice and there are even more opinions about how to do so! Much, of course, depends on the variety and brand of rice being used, the dish being prepared and the desired results. Each variety of rice has its own characteristics. Some types of rice cook to light, separate grains; some to a rich, creamy consistency; and some to a consistency where the grains stick together. It is important, therefore, to ensure that the appropriate rice is used. Different types of rice have very different powers of absorption. Long-grain rice will absorb about three times its weight in water, whereas just 25 g/1 oz of plump and short-grained pudding rice can soak up a massive 300 ml/½ pint of liquid.

COOKING LONG-GRAIN RICE

By far the simplest method of cooking long-grain rice – whether white, brown or basmati – is to add it to plenty of boiling, salted water in a large saucepan, so that the rice grains can move freely and do not stick together. Allow about 50 g/2 oz of rice per person when cooking as an accompaniment. Rinse it under cold, running water until clear – this removes any starch still clinging to the grains – then tip into the rapidly boiling water. Stir once, then when the water comes back to the boil, turn down the heat a little and simmer uncovered, allowing 10–12 minutes for white rice and 30–40 minutes for brown (check the packet timings, as brands of rice vary). The easiest way to test if the rice is cooked is to bite a couple of grains – they should be tender but still firm. Drain the rice straight away, then return to the pan with a little butter and herbs if liked. Fluff the grains with a fork and serve. If you need to keep the rice warm, put it in a bowl and place over a pan of barely simmering water. Cover the top of the bowl with a clean tea towel until ready to serve.

ABSORPTION METHOD

Cooking rice using the absorption method is also very simple and is favoured by many because no draining is involved and therefore no water is wasted. Also, by using this method, stock and other flavourful ingredients can be added and will be absorbed by the rice. Furthermore,

valuable nutrients are retained that would otherwise be lost in the cooking water when drained. To cook rice this way, weigh out the quantity of rice you require, then measure it by volume in a measuring jug – you will need about 150 ml/¼ pint for two people. Briefly rinse the rice in a sieve under cold running water, then tip into a large heavy-based saucepan. If liked, you can cook the rice in a little butter or oil for about 1 minute. Pour in two parts water to one part rice (or use stock if you prefer), season with salt and bring to the boil uncovered. Cover the pan with a tight-fitting lid, then simmer gently without lifting the lid, until the liquid is absorbed and the rice is tender. White rice will take 15 minutes to cook, whereas brown rice will take about 35 minutes. It is important to simmer over a very low heat or the liquid will cook away before the rice is ready. Do not be tempted to check the rice too often while it is cooking as you will let out steam and therefore moisture. If there is still a little liquid

left when the rice is tender, remove the lid and cook for about a minute until evaporated. Remove from the heat and leave to stand with the lid on for 4–5 minutes. Do not rinse the rice when it is cooked, just fluff up with a fork before serving. This method is also good for cooking Jasmine and Valencia rice.

OVEN-BAKED METHOD

The oven-baked method also works by absorption. It takes a little longer than cooking rice on the hob, but is ideal to add to the oven if you are roasting or simmering a casserole.

To make oven-baked rice for two people, gently fry a chopped onion in 1 tablespoon of olive oil in a 1.1 litre/ 2 pint flameproof casserole dish until soft and golden (leave the onion out if preferred). Add 75 g/3 oz long-grain rice and cook for 1 minute, then stir in 300 ml/ ½ pint of stock – you can also add a finely pared strip of lemon rind or a bay leaf at this stage. Cover with a lid or tinfoil and bake on the middle shelf of a preheated oven at 180°C/ 350°F/Gas Mark 4 for 40 minutes, or until the rice is tender and all the stock has been absorbed. Fluff up with a fork before serving.

COOKING IN THE MICROWAVE

Rinse long-grain white or brown rice in cold running water, then place in a large heat-proof bowl. Add boiling water or stock to the bowl, allowing 300 ml/½ pint for 125 g/4 oz rice and 550 ml/18 fl oz for 225 g/8 oz rice. Add a pinch of salt and a knob of butter, if desired. Cover with clingfilm, making a few air holes to allow the steam to escape and microwave on high for 3 minutes. Stir, then re-cover and microwave on medium for 12 minutes for white rice and 25 minutes for brown. Leave to stand, covered, for 5 minutes before fluffing up with a fork and serving.

IN A PRESSURE COOKER

Follow the quantities given for the absorption method and bring to the boil in the pressure cooker. Stir once, cover with the lid and bring to a high 6.8 kg/15 lb pressure. Lower the heat and cook for 5 minutes if white rice or cook for 8 minutes if brown rice.

IN A RICE COOKER

Follow the quantities given for the absorption method. Put the rice, salt and boiling water or stock in the cooker, bring back to the boil and cover. When all the liquid has been absorbed the cooker will turn itself off automatically.

WILD RICE

This type of rice can be cooked by any of the methods used for long-grain rice, but the cooking time required is longer. It will take between 35–50 minutes to cook wild rice, depending on whether you like your rice slightly chewy or very tender. To speed up the cooking time by 5–10 minutes, soak the rice in cold water first for 30 minutes. This also increases the volume of the rice when it is cooked.

RED RICE

Cook this in the same way as brown rice as this type of rice has a very hard grain. It is best to cook the rice for about 40–60 minutes if you like your rice really tender – it will still keep its shape.

RISOTTO RICE

Most rices should not be stirred during cooking as it breaks up the grains and makes them soggy. Risotto rice is different as it can absorb nearly five times its weight in liquid and still retains its shape. A good risotto has a creamy texture, with a slight bite to the individual grains and is made by adding the cooking liquid gradually and stirring almost continuously during cooking.

For a classic risotto (known as alla Milanese) for four people, place 1 tablespoon of olive oil and a knob of butter in a large heavy-based saucepan. Slowly heat the butter and oil until the butter has melted. Add 1 chopped onion to the pan and cook until tender. Add 150 ml/¼ pint of dry white wine and boil rapidly until almost totally reduced. Stir in 300 g/11 oz risotto rice. Add 1 litre/1¾ pints boiling vegetable or chicken stock, a ladleful at a time – each ladleful should be completely absorbed by the rice before the next one is added. Continue adding the stock until the rice is tender. This will take 15–20 minutes, although it may not be necessary to add all of the stock to achieve the desired consistency. Serve the risotto straight away, sprinkled with grated Parmesan cheese. The basic risotto can be flavoured in many ways. Try adding a couple of bay leaves, a lemon grass stalk or a large pinch of saffron to the stock, or use more red or white wine and less stock.

GLUTINOUS RICE

This rice is steamed (instead of being cooked in boiling water) until the grains are soft, tender and stick together in a mass. Cooking times vary slightly according to the brand, so check the packet instructions for specific directions.

PUDDING RICE

For a simple rice pudding put 50 g/2 oz of pudding rice in a buttered 1.2 litre/2 pint oven-proof dish with sugar to taste. Pour over 600 ml/1 pint of near-boiling milk and bake in a preheated oven at 150°C/300°F/Gas Mark 2 for 30 minutes. Stir, then bake for a further 1–1¼ hours until tender. Vary the flavour by infusing the milk with orange rind, adding nuts and dried fruit to the mixture or using 300 ml/½ pint coconut milk or single cream and 300 ml/½ pint of milk instead of milk alone.

HEALTH AND NUTRITION

Rice has been the dietary staple of the East for centuries where it has provided a healthy, balanced diet and has added substance to the small quantities of meat used in Eastern cooking. It is low in fat and high in complex carbohydrates which are absorbed slowly, helping to maintain blood sugar levels. Rice is also a reasonable source of protein and provides most of the B vitamins and the minerals potassium and phosphorus. It is also a gluten-free cereal, making it suitable for coeliacs. Like other unrefined grains, brown rice is richer in nutrients and fibre than refined white rice.

HERBS AND SPICES

Herbs are easy to grow and a garden is not needed as they can easily thrive on a small patio, window box or even on a windowsill. It is worth the effort to plant a few herbs as they do not require much attention or nurturing. The reward will be a range of fresh herbs available whenever needed and fresh flavours which cannot be beaten to add to any dish that is being prepared.

While fresh herbs should be picked or bought as close as possible to the time of use, freeze-dried and dried herbs and spices will usually keep for around six months.

The best idea is to buy little and often, and to store the herbs in airtight jars in a cool dark cupboard. Fresh herbs tend to have a milder flavour than dried and equate to around one level tablespoon of fresh to one level teaspoon of dried. As a result, quantities used in cooking should be altered accordingly. A variety of herbs and spices and their uses are listed below.

ALLSPICE

The dark allspice berries come whole or ground and have a flavour similar to that of cinnamon, cloves and nutmeg. Although not the same as mixed spices, allspice can be used with pickles, relishes, cakes and milk puddings or whole in meat and fish dishes.

ANISEED

Aniseed comes in whole seeds or ground. It has a strong aroma and flavour and should be used sparingly in baking and salad dressings.

BASIL

Best fresh but also available in dried form, basil can be used raw or cooked. It works well in many dishes but is particularly well suited to tomato-based dishes and sauces, salads and Mediterranean recipes.

BAY LEAVES

Bay leaves are available in fresh or dried form as well as ground. They make up part of a bouquet garni and are particularly delicious when added to meat and poultry dishes, soups, stews, vegetable dishes and stuffing. They also impart a spicy flavour to milk puddings and egg custards.

BOUQUET GARNI

Bouquet garni is a bouquet of fresh herbs tied with a piece of string or in a small piece of muslin. It is used to flavour casseroles, stews and stocks or sauces. The herbs that are normally used are parsley, thyme, and bay leaves.

CARAWAY SEEDS

Caraway seeds have a warm sweet taste and are often used in breads and cakes but are delicious with cabbage dishes and pickles as well.

CAYENNE

Cayenne is the powdered form of a red chilli pepper said to be native to Cayenne. It is similar in appearance to paprika and can be used sparingly to add a fiery kick to many dishes.

CARDAMOM

Cardamom has a distinctive sweet, rich taste and can be bought whole in the pod, in seed form or ground. This sweet aromatic spice is delicious in curries, rice, cakes and biscuits and is great served with rice pudding and fruit.

CHERVIL

Reminiscent of parsley and available either in fresh or dried form, chervil has a faintly sweet, spicy flavour and is particularly good in soups, cheese dishes, stews and with eggs.

CHILLI

Available whole, fresh, dried and in powdered form, red chillies tend to be sweeter in taste than their green counterparts. They are particularly associated with Spanish and Mexican-style cooking and curries, but are also delicious with pickles, dips, sauces and in pizza toppings.

CHIVES

Best used when fresh but also available in dried form, this member of the onion family is ideal for use when a delicate onion flavour is required. Chives are good with eggs, cheese, fish and vegetable dishes. They also work well as a garnish for soups, meat and vegetable dishes.

CINNAMON

Cinnamon comes in the form of reddish-brown sticks of bark from an evergreen tree and has a sweet, pungent aroma. Either whole or ground, cinnamon is delicious in cakes and milk puddings, particularly with apple, and is used in mulled wine and for preserving.

CLOVES

Mainly used whole although also available ground, cloves have a very warm, sweet pungent aroma and can be used to stud roast ham and pork, in mulled wine and punch and when pickling fruit. When ground, they can be used in making mincemeat and in Christmas puddings and biscuits.

CORIANDER

Coriander seeds have an orangey flavour and are available whole or ground. Coriander is particularly delicious (whether whole or roughly ground) in casseroles, curries and as a pickling spice. The leaves are used to flavour spicy aromatic dishes as well as a garnish.

CUMIN

Also available ground or as whole seeds, cumin has a strong, slightly bitter flavour. It is one of the main ingredients in curry powder and compliments many fish, meat and rice dishes.

DILL

Dill leaves are available fresh or dried and have a mild flavour, while the seeds are slightly bitter. Dill is particularly good with salmon, new potatoes and in sauces. The seeds are good in pickles and vegetable dishes.

FENNEL

Whole seeds or ground, fennel has a fragrant, sweet aniseed flavour and is sometimes known as the fish herb because it compliments fish dishes so well.

GINGER

Ginger comes in many forms but primarily as a fresh root and in dried ground form, which can be used in baking, curries, pickles, sauces and Chinese cooking.

LEMON GRASS

Available fresh and dried, with a subtle, aromatic, lemony flavour, lemon grass is essential to Thai cooking. It is also delicious when added to soups, poultry and fish dishes.

MACE

The outer husk of nutmeg has a milder nutmeg flavour and can be used in pickles, cheese dishes, stewed fruits, sauces and hot punch.

MARJORAM

Often dried, marjoram has a sweet slightly spicy flavour, which tastes fantastic when added to stuffing, meat or tomato-based dishes.

MINT

Available fresh or dried, mint has a strong, sweet aroma which is delicious in a sauce or jelly to serve with lamb. It is also great with fresh peas and new potatoes and is an essential ingredient in Pimms.

MUSTARD SEED

These yellow and brown seeds are available whole or ground and are often found in pickles, relishes, cheese dishes, dressings, curries and as an accompaniment to meat.

NUTMEG

The large whole seeds have a warm, sweet taste and compliment custards, milk puddings, cheese dishes, parsnips and creamy soups.

OREGANO

The strongly flavoured dried leaves of oregano are similar to marjoram and are used extensively in Italian and Greek cooking.

PAPRIKA

Paprika often comes in two varieties. One is quite sweet and mild and the other has a slight bite to it. Paprika is made from the fruit of the sweet pepper and is good in meat and poultry dishes as well as a garnish. The rule of buying herbs and spices little and often applies particularly to paprika as unfortunately it does not keep particularly well.

PARSLEY

The stems as well as the leaves of parsley can be used to compliment most savoury dishes as they contain the most flavour. They can also be used as a garnish.

PEPPER

This comes in white and black peppercorns and is best freshly ground. Both add flavour to most dishes, sauces and gravies. Black pepper has a more robust flavour, while white pepper is much more delicate.

POPPY SEEDS

These little, grey-black coloured seeds impart a sweet, nutty flavour when added to biscuits, vegetable dishes, dressings and cheese dishes.

ROSEMARY

Delicious fresh or dried, these small, needle-like leaves have a sweet aroma which is particularly good with lamb, stuffing and vegetables dishes. Also delicious when added to charcoal on the barbecue to give a piquant flavour to meat and corn on the cob.

SAFFRON

Deep orange in colour, saffron is traditionally used in paella, rice and cakes but is also delicious with poultry. Saffron is the most expensive of all spices.

SAGE

Fresh or dried sage leaves have a pungent, slightly bitter taste which is delicious with pork and poultry, sausages, stuffing and with stuffed pasta when tossed in a little butter and fresh sage.

SAVORY

This herb resembles thyme, but has a softer flavour that particularly compliments all types of fish and beans.

SESAME

Sesame seeds have a nutty taste, especially when toasted, and are delicious in baking, on salads, or with far-eastern cooking.

TARRAGON

The fresh or dried leaves of tarragon have a sweet aromatic taste which is particularly good with poultry, seafood, fish, creamy sauces and stuffing.

THYME

Available fresh or dried, thyme has a pungent flavour and is included in bouquet garni. It compliments many meat and poultry dishes and stuffing.

TURMERIC

Turmeric is obtained from the root of a lily from southeast Asia. This root is ground and has a brilliant yellow colour. It has a bitter, peppery flavour and is often combined for use in curry powder and mustard. Also delicious in pickles, relishes and dressings.

RICE & TOMATO SOUP

INGREDIENTS   Serves 4

150 g/5 oz easy-cook basmati
  rice
400 g can chopped tomatoes
2 garlic cloves, peeled and
  crushed
grated rind of ½ lime
2 tbsp extra-virgin olive oil
1 tsp sugar
salt and freshly ground pepper

300 ml/½ pint vegetable stock
  or water

FOR THE CROÛTONS:
2 tbsp prepared pesto sauce
2 tbsp olive oil
6 thin slices ciabatta bread,
  cut into 1 cm/½ inch cubes

1 Preheat the oven to 220°C/
425°F/Gas Mark 7. Rinse
and drain the basmati rice. Place
the canned tomatoes with their
juice in a large heavy-based
saucepan with the garlic, lime
rind, oil and sugar. Season to
taste with salt and pepper. Bring
to the boil, then reduce the heat,
cover and simmer for 10 minutes.

2 Add the boiling vegetable
stock or water and the rice,
then cook, uncovered, for a
further 15–20 minutes, or until
the rice is tender. If the soup
is too thick, add a little more
water. Reserve and keep warm,
if the croutons are not ready.

3 Meanwhile, to make the
croutons, mix the pesto and
olive oil in a large bowl. Add the
bread cubes and toss until they
are coated completely with the
mixture. Spread on a baking
sheet and bake in the preheated
oven for 10–15 minutes, until
golden and crisp, turning them

over halfway through cooking.
Serve the soup immediately
sprinkled with the warm croutons.

HELPFUL HINT

Pesto is a vivid green sauce,
made from basil leaves and
olive oil. Shop-bought pesto
is fine for this quick soup, but
try making your own during
the summer when basil is
plentiful. To make 150 ml/
¼ pint of pesto, put 25 g/1 oz
fresh basil leaves (weighed
without stalks), 1 peeled garlic
clove, 1 tablespoon pine
nuts, 4 tablespoons olive oil,
salt and black pepper in a
blender or food processor
and blend together at high
speed until very creamy. Stir
in 25 g/1 oz freshly grated
Parmesan cheese. Store in
the refrigerator for up to 2
weeks in a screw-topped jar.

RICH TOMATO SOUP WITH ROASTED RED PEPPERS

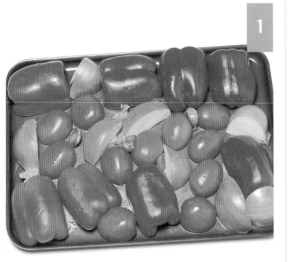

INGREDIENTS   Serves 4

2 tsp light olive oil
700 g/1½ lb red peppers,
   halved and deseeded
450 g/1 lb ripe plum tomatoes,
   halved
2 onions, unpeeled and
   quartered

4 garlic cloves, unpeeled
600 ml/1 pint chicken stock
salt and freshly ground black
   pepper
4 tbsp soured cream
1 tbsp freshly shredded basil

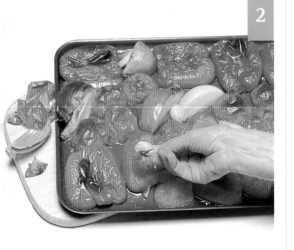

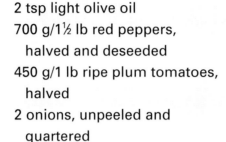

1 Preheat oven to 200°C/ 400°F/Gas Mark 6. Lightly oil a roasting tin with 1 teaspoon of the olive oil. Place the peppers and tomatoes cut side down in the roasting tin with the onion quarters and the garlic cloves. Spoon over the remaining oil.

2 Bake in the preheated oven for 30 minutes, or until the skins on the peppers have started to blacken and blister. Allow the vegetables to cool for about 10 minutes, then remove the skins, stalks and seeds from the peppers. Peel away the skins from the tomatoes and onions and squeeze out the garlic.

3 Place the cooked vegetables into a blender or food processor and blend until smooth. Add the stock and blend again to form a smooth purée. Pour the puréed soup through a sieve, if a smooth soup is preferred, then pour into a saucepan. Bring to the boil, simmer gently for 2–3 minutes, and season to taste with salt and pepper. Serve hot with a swirl of soured cream and a sprinkling of shredded basil on the top.

TASTY TIP

To help remove the skins of the peppers more easily, remove them from the oven and put immediately into a plastic bag or a bowl covered with clingfilm. Leave until cool enough to handle then skin carefully.

HOT & SOUR MUSHROOM SOUP

INGREDIENTS   Serves 4

4 tbsp sunflower oil
3 garlic cloves, peeled and
   finely chopped
3 shallots, peeled and finely
   chopped
2 large red chillies, deseeded
   and finely chopped
1 tbsp soft brown sugar
large pinch of salt
1 litre/1¾ pints vegetable stock
250 g/9 oz Thai fragrant rice
5 kaffir lime leaves, torn
2 tbsp soy sauce

grated rind and juice of 1
   lemon
250 g/9 oz oyster mushrooms,
   wiped and cut into pieces
2 tbsp freshly chopped
   coriander

TO GARNISH:
2 green chillies, deseeded and
   finely chopped
3 spring onions, trimmed and
   finely chopped

1 Heat the oil in a frying pan, add the garlic and shallots and cook until golden brown and starting to crisp. Remove from the pan and reserve. Add the chillies to the pan and cook until they start to change colour.

2 Place the garlic, shallots and chillies in a food processor or blender and blend to a smooth purée with 150 ml /¼ pint water. Pour the purée back into the pan, add the sugar with a large pinch of salt, then cook gently, stirring, until dark in colour. Take care not to burn the mixture.

3 Pour the stock into a large saucepan, add the garlic purée, rice, lime leaves, soy sauce and the lemon rind and juice. Bring to the boil, then reduce the heat, cover and simmer gently for about 10 minutes.

4 Add the mushrooms and simmer for a further 10 minutes, or until the mushrooms and rice are tender. Remove the lime leaves, stir in the chopped coriander and ladle into bowls. Place the chopped green chillies and spring onions in small bowls and serve separately to sprinkle on top of the soup.

HELPFUL HINT

There are many kinds of chilli, varying in both size and colour, but they all have a hot, spicy flavour. They contain volatile oils which can irritate your skin, so during preparation take great care not to touch your eyes and wash your hands immediately after handling.

CHINESE LEAF & MUSHROOM SOUP

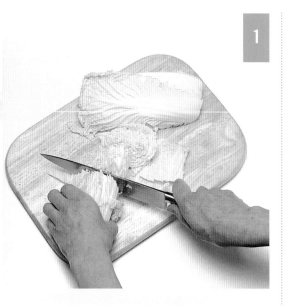

INGREDIENTS   Serves 4–6

450 g/1 lb Chinese leaves
25 g/1 oz dried Chinese
    (shiitake) mushrooms
1 tbsp vegetable oil
75 g/3 oz smoked streaky
    bacon, diced
2.5 cm/1 inch piece fresh root
    ginger, peeled and finely
    chopped
175 g/6 oz chestnut
    mushrooms, thinly sliced

1.1 litres/2 pints chicken stock
4–6 spring onions, trimmed
    and cut into short lengths
2 tbsp dry sherry or Chinese
    rice wine
salt and freshly ground black
    pepper
sesame oil for drizzling

1 Trim the stem ends of the Chinese leaves and cut in half lengthways. Remove the triangular core with a knife, then cut into 2.5 cm/1 inch slices and reserve.

2 Place the dried Chinese mushrooms in a bowl and pour over enough almost boiling water to cover. Leave to stand for 20 minutes to soften, then gently lift out and squeeze out the liquid. Discard the stems and thinly slice the caps and reserve. Strain the liquid through a muslin-lined sieve or a coffee filter paper and reserve.

3 Heat a wok over a medium-high heat, add the oil and when hot add the bacon. Stir-fry for 3–4 minutes, or until crisp and golden, stirring frequently. Add the ginger and chestnut mushrooms and stir-fry for a further 2–3 minutes.

4 Add the chicken stock and bring to the boil, skimming any fat and scum that rises to the surface. Add the spring onions, sherry or rice wine, Chinese leaves, sliced Chinese mushrooms and season to taste with salt and pepper. Pour in the reserved soaking liquid and reduce the heat to the lowest possible setting.

5 Simmer gently, covered, until all the vegetables are very tender; this will take about 10 minutes. Add a little water if the liquid has reduced too much. Spoon into soup bowls and drizzle with a little sesame oil. Serve immediately.

TASTY TIP

If Chinese leaves are not available, use Savoy cabbage.

CHINESE CHICKEN SOUP

INGREDIENTS   Serves 4

225 g/8 oz cooked chicken
1 tsp oil
6 spring onions, trimmed
   and diagonally sliced
1 red chilli, deseeded
   and finely chopped
1 garlic clove, peeled
   and crushed
2.5 cm/1 inch piece
   root ginger, peeled
   and finely grated

1 litre/1¾ pint chicken stock
150 g/5 oz medium
   egg noodles
1 carrot, peeled and cut
   into matchsticks
125 g/4 oz beansprouts
2 tbsp soy sauce
1 tbsp fish sauce
fresh coriander leaves,
   to garnish

1 Remove any skin from the chicken. Place on a chopping board and use two forks to tear the chicken into fine shreds.

2 Heat the oil in a large saucepan and fry the spring onions and chilli for 1 minute.

3 Add the garlic and ginger and cook for another minute.

4 Stir in the chicken stock and gradually bring the mixture to the boil.

5 Break up the noodles a little and add to the boiling stock with the carrot.

6 Stir to mix, then reduce the heat to a simmer and cook for 3–4 minutes.

7 Add the shredded chicken, beansprouts, soy sauce and fish sauce and stir.

8 Cook for a further 2–3 minutes until piping hot. Ladle the soup into bowls and sprinkle with the coriander leaves. Serve immediately.

TASTY TIP

If possible, buy corn-fed chicken for this recipe. Since this soup is chicken stock-based, the use of corn-fed chicken will make the soup much more flavoursome. For added nutritional value, substitute the egg noodles with the wholewheat variety and use sesame oil in step 2. Increase the vegetable content by adding 75 g/3 oz each of water chestnuts and bamboo shoots and 50 g/2 oz of sugar snap peas and baby corn in step 7.

PUMPKIN & SMOKED ADDOCK SOUP

1

INGREDIENTS
Serves 4–6

2 tbsp olive oil

1 medium onion, peeled and chopped

2 garlic cloves, peeled and chopped

3 celery stalks, trimmed and chopped

700 g/1½ lb pumpkin, peeled, deseeded and cut into chunks

450 g/1 lb potatoes, peeled and cut into chunks

750 ml/1¼ pints chicken stock, heated

125 ml/4 fl oz dry sherry

200 g/7 oz smoked haddock fillet

150 ml/¼ pint milk

freshly ground black pepper

2 tbsp freshly chopped parsley

4

5

1 Heat the oil in a large heavy-based saucepan and gently cook the onion, garlic, and celery for about 10 minutes. This will release the sweetness but not colour the vegetables. Add the pumpkin and potatoes to the saucepan and stir to coat the vegetables with the oil.

2 Gradually pour in the stock and bring to the boil. Cover, then reduce the heat and simmer for 25 minutes, stirring occasionally. Stir in the dry sherry, then remove the saucepan from the heat and leave to cool for 5–10 minutes.

3 Blend the mixture in a food processor or blender to form a chunky purée and return to the cleaned saucepan.

4 Meanwhile, place the fish in a shallow frying pan. Pour in

the milk with 3 tablespoons of water and bring to almost boiling point. Reduce the heat, cover and simmer for 6 minutes, or until the fish is cooked and flakes easily. Remove from the heat and, using a slotted spoon remove the fish from the liquid, reserving both liquid and fish.

5 Discard the skin and any bones from the fish and flake into pieces. Stir the fish liquid into the soup, together with the flaked fish. Season with freshly ground black pepper, stir in the parsley and serve immediately.

TASTY TIP

Try to find undyed smoked haddock for this soup rather than the brightly coloured yellow type, as the texture and flavour is better.

PASTA & BEAN SOUP

INGREDIENTS   Serves 4–6

3 tbsp olive oil

2 celery sticks, trimmed and finely chopped

100 g/3½ oz prosciutto or prosciutto di speck, cut in pieces

1 red chilli, deseeded and finely chopped

2 large potatoes, peeled and cut into 2.5 cm/1 in cubes

2 garlic cloves, peeled and finely chopped

3 ripe plum tomatoes, skinned and chopped

1 x 400 g cans borlotti beans, drained and rinsed

1 litre/1¾ pints chicken or vegetable stock

100 g/3½ oz pasta shapes

large handful basil leaves, torn

salt and freshly ground black pepper

shredded basil leaves, to garnish

crusty bread, to serve

1 Heat the olive oil in a heavy-based pan, add the celery and prosciutto and cook gently for 6–8 minutes, or until softened. Add the chopped chilli and potato cubes and cook for a further 10 minutes.

2 Add the garlic to the chilli and potato mixture and cook for 1 minute. Add the chopped tomatoes and simmer for 5 minutes. Stir in two-thirds of the beans, then pour in the chicken or vegetable stock and bring to the boil.

3 Add the pasta shapes to the soup stock and return it to simmering point. Cook the pasta for about 10 minutes, or until 'al dente'.

4 Meanwhile, place the remaining beans in a food processor or blender and blend with enough of the soup stock to make a smooth, thinnish purée.

5 When the pasta is cooked, stir in the puréed beans with the torn basil. Season the soup to taste with salt and pepper. Ladle into serving bowls, garnish with shredded basil and serve immediately with plenty of crusty bread.

HELPFUL HINT

Oval borlotti beans have red-streaked, pinkish-brown skin. They have a moist texture and a bitter-sweet flavour, which makes them excellent in soups. Pinto beans and cannellini beans are good alternatives.

CHICKEN NOODLE SOUP

INGREDIENTS   Serves 4

carcass of a medium-sized
  cooked chicken
1 large carrot, peeled and
  roughly chopped
1 medium onion, peeled and
  quartered
1 leek, trimmed and roughly
  chopped
2–3 bay leaves
a few black peppercorns
2 litres/3½ pints water

225 g/8 oz Chinese cabbage,
  trimmed
50 g/2 oz chestnut
  mushrooms, wiped and
  sliced
125 g/4 oz cooked chicken,
  sliced or chopped
50 g/2 oz medium or fine egg
  thread noodles

1 Break the chicken carcass into smaller pieces and place in the wok with the carrot, onion, leek, bay leaves, peppercorns and water. Bring slowly to the boil. Skim away any fat or scum that rises for the first 15 minutes. Simmer very gently for 1–1½ hours. If the liquid reduces by more than one third, add a little more water.

2 Remove from the heat and leave until cold. Strain into a large bowl and chill in the refrigerator until any fat in the stock rises and sets on the surface. Remove the fat and discard. Draw a sheet of absorbent kitchen paper across the surface of the stock to absorb any remaining fat.

3 Return the stock to the wok and bring to a simmer. Add the Chinese cabbage, mushrooms and chicken and simmer gently

for 7–8 minutes until the vegetables are tender.

4 Meanwhile, cook the noodles according to the packet directions until tender. Drain well. Transfer a portion of noodles to each serving bowl before pouring in some soup and vegetables. Serve immediately.

HELPFUL HINT

This is an excellent way to use up any leftover chicken as well as the carcass from a roast chicken.

BRUSCHETTA WITH PECORINO, GARLIC & TOMATOES

1

INGREDIENTS   Serves 4

6 ripe but firm tomatoes
125 g/4 oz pecorino cheese,
  finely grated
1 tbsp oregano leaves
salt and freshly ground black
  pepper
3 tbsp olive oil

3 garlic cloves, peeled
8 slices of flat Italian bread,
  such as focaccia
50 g/2 oz mozzarella cheese
marinated black olives,
  to serve

2

1 Preheat grill and line the grill rack with tinfoil just before cooking. Make a small cross in the top of the tomatoes, then place in a small bowl and cover with boiling water. Leave to stand for 2 minutes, then drain and remove the skins. Cut into quarters, remove the seeds, and chop the flesh into small dice.

2 Mix the tomato flesh with the pecorino cheese and 2 teaspoons of the fresh oregano and season to taste with salt and pepper. Add 1 tablespoon of the olive oil and mix thoroughly.

3

3 Crush the garlic and spread evenly over the slices of bread. Heat 2 tablespoons of the olive oil in a large frying pan and sauté the bread slices until they are crisp and golden.

4 Place the fried bread on a lightly oiled baking tray and spoon on the tomato and cheese topping. Place a little mozzarella on top and place under the preheated grill for 3–4 minutes, until golden and bubbling. Garnish with the remaining oregano, then arrange the bruschettas on a serving plate and serve immediately with the olives.

TASTY TIP

Bitter leaves are excellent with these bruschettas because they help to offset the richness of the cheese and tomato topping. Try a mixture of frisée, radicchio and rocket. If these are unavailable, use a bag of mixed salad leaves.

STUFFED VINE LEAVES

INGREDIENTS   Serves 6–8

150 g/5 oz long-grain rice

225 g/8 oz fresh or preserved vine leaves

225 g/8 oz red onion, peeled and finely chopped

3 baby leeks, trimmed and finely sliced

25 g/1 oz freshly chopped parsley

25 g/1 oz freshly chopped mint

25 g/1 oz freshly chopped dill

150 ml/¼ pint extra-virgin olive oil

salt and freshly ground black pepper

50 g/2 oz currants

50 g/2 oz ready-to-eat dried apricots, finely chopped

25 g/1 oz pine nuts

juice of 1 lemon

600–750 ml/1–1¼ pints boiling stock

lemon wedges or slices, to garnish

4 tbsp Greek-style yogurt, to serve

1 Soak the rice in cold water for 30 minutes. If using fresh vine leaves, blanch 5–6 leaves at a time, in salted boiling water for a minute. Rinse and drain. If using preserved vine leaves, soak in tepid water for at least 20 minutes, drain, rinse and pat dry with absorbent kitchen paper.

2 Mix the onion and leeks with the herbs and half the oil. Add the drained rice, mix and season to taste with salt and pepper. Stir in the currants, apricots, pine nuts and lemon juice. Spoon 1 teaspoon of the filling at the stalk end of each leaf. Roll, tucking the side flaps into the centre to create a neat parcel; do not roll too tight. Continue until all the filling is used.

3 Layer half the remaining vine leaves over the base of a large frying pan. Pack the little parcels in the frying pan and cover with the remaining leaves.

4 Pour in enough stock to just cover the vine leaves, add a pinch of salt and bring to the boil. Reduce the heat, cover and simmer for 45–55 minutes, or until the rice is sticky and tender. Leave to stand for 10 minutes. Drain the stock. Garnish with lemon wedges and serve hot with the Greek yogurt.

FOOD FACT

The use of vine leaves in cooking goes back as far as the early cultivation of vines. Particularly popular in Middle Eastern cooking, they give a delicious, tart, grapey flavour to dishes.

HOT HERBY MUSHROOMS

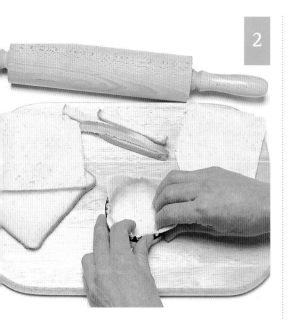

INGREDIENTS   Serves 4

4 thin slices of white bread,
  crusts removed
125 g/4 oz chestnut
  mushrooms, wiped
  and sliced
125 g/4 oz oyster
  mushrooms, wiped
1 garlic clove, peeled
  and crushed

1 tsp Dijon mustard
300 ml/½ pint chicken stock
 salt and freshly ground
  black pepper
1 tbsp freshly chopped parsley
1 tbsp freshly snipped chives,
  plus extra to garnish
mixed salad leaves, to serve

1 Preheat the oven to 180°C/350°F/Gas Mark 4. With a rolling pin, roll each piece of bread out as thinly as possible.

2 Press each piece of bread into a 10 cm/4 inch tartlet tin. Push each piece firmly down, then bake in the preheated oven for 20 minutes.

3 Place the mushrooms in a frying pan with the garlic, mustard and chicken stock and stir-fry over a moderate heat until the mushrooms are tender and the liquid is reduced by half.

4 Carefully remove the mushrooms from the frying pan with a slotted spoon and transfer to a heat-resistant dish. Cover with tinfoil and place in the bottom of the oven to keep the mushrooms warm.

5 Boil the remaining pan juices until reduced to a thick sauce. Season with salt and pepper.

6 Stir the parsley and the chives into the mushroom mixture.

7 Place one bread tartlet case on each plate and divide the mushroom mixture between them.

8 Spoon over the pan juices, garnish with the chives and serve immediately with mixed salad leaves.

FOOD FACT

Mushrooms are an extremely nutritious food, rich in vitamins and minerals, which help to boost our immune system. This recipe could be adapted to include shiitake mushrooms which studies have shown can significantly boost and protect the body's immune system and can go some way to boost the body's protection against cancer.

SMOKED SALMON SUSHI

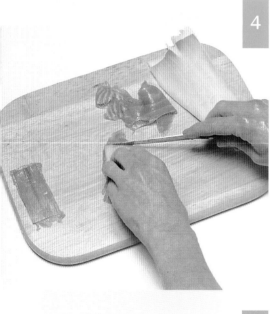

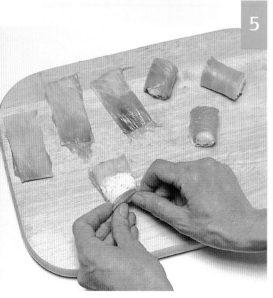

INGREDIENTS   Serves 4

125 g/4 oz sushi rice or round
   pudding rice
2 tbsp cider vinegar
1 tbsp caster sugar
1 tsp salt
2 green leeks, trimmed

225 g/8 oz smoked salmon
1 tsp Japanese soy sauce

TO GARNISH:
few fresh chives
lemon or lime wedges

1 Wash the rice in plenty of cold water, then drain. Put the rice and 200 ml/7 fl oz cold water in a saucepan and leave to soak for 30 minutes. Place the saucepan over a medium heat and bring to the boil, stirring frequently. Lower the heat, cover and cook the rice for about 15 minutes, or until the grains are tender and the water has been absorbed. Remove from the heat and leave, still covered, for a further 10–15 minutes.

2 Place the vinegar, sugar and salt in a small saucepan. Heat gently, stirring to dissolve the sugar. Turn the rice into a large bowl, sprinkle over the vinegar mixture and mix through the rice.

3 Cut the trimmed leeks in half lengthways, then blanch in boiling water for 3–4 minutes. Drain and place in ice-cold water for 5 minutes, then drain.

4 Separate the leek leaves. Cut both the leek leaves and the salmon slices lengthways into 2.5 x 7.5 cm (1 x 3 inch) strips,

reserving 2 wide leek leaves. Place the leek slices neatly on top of the sliced salmon.

5 Spoon the rice onto the salmon and leek slices, then roll into parcels. Using the tip of a sharp knife, slice the reserved leek leaves lengthways into long strips. Tie the strips around the smoked salmon parcels. Sprinkle the parcels with a few drops of the soy sauce, garnish with the chives and lemon wedges and serve.

FOOD FACT

It takes many years of training to qualify as a sushi chef, but these smoked salmon and leek canapes are simple to make, although a little time-consuming. Rolled sushi like these are known as Hosomaki in Japan. Use the rice straight away after cooking – it cannot be stored in the refrigerator or it will harden and be difficult to work with.

ORIENTAL MINCED CHICKEN ON OCKET & TOMATO

INGREDIENTS — Serves 4

2 shallots, peeled
1 garlic clove, peeled
1 carrot, peeled
50 g/2 oz water chestnuts
1 tsp oil
350 g/12 oz fresh
  chicken mince

1 tsp Chinese five-spice
  powder
pinch chilli powder
1 tsp soy sauce
1 tbsp fish sauce
8 cherry tomatoes
50 g/2 oz rocket

1 Finely chop the shallots and garlic. Cut the carrot into matchsticks, thinly slice the water chestnuts and reserve. Heat the oil in a wok or heavy-based large frying pan and add the chicken. Stir-fry for 3–4 minutes over a moderately high heat, breaking up any large pieces of chicken.

2 Add the garlic and shallots and cook for 2–3 minutes until softened. Sprinkle over the Chinese five-spice powder and the chilli powder and continue to cook for about 1 minute.

3 Add the carrot, water chestnuts, soy and fish sauce and 2 tablespoons of water. Stir-fry for a further 2 minutes. Remove from the heat and reserve to cool slightly.

4 Deseed the tomatoes and cut into thin wedges. Toss with the rocket and divide between 4 serving plates. Spoon the warm chicken mixture over the rocket and tomato wedges and serve immediately to prevent the rocket from wilting.

TASTY TIP

This is a very versatile dish. In place of the chicken you could use any lean cut of meat or even prawns. To make this dish a main meal replace the rocket and tomatoes with stir-fried vegetables and rice. Another alternative that works very well is to serve the chicken mixture in step 3 in lettuce leaves. Place a spoonful of the mixture into a lettuce leaf and roll up into a small parcel.

ITALIAN BAKED TOMATOES WITH CURLY ENDIVE & RADICCHIO

INGREDIENTS   Serves 4

1 tsp olive oil
4 beef tomatoes
salt
50 g/2 oz fresh white
  breadcrumbs
1 tbsp freshly snipped chives
1 tbsp freshly chopped parsley
125 g/4 oz button mushrooms,
  finely chopped
salt and freshly ground black
  pepper

25 g/1 oz fresh Parmesan
  cheese, grated

FOR THE SALAD:
½ curly endive lettuce
½ small piece of radicchio
2 tbsp olive oil
1 tsp balsamic vinegar
salt and freshly ground black
  pepper

1 Preheat oven to 190°C/ 375°F/Gas Mark 5. Lightly oil a baking tray with the teaspoon of oil. Slice the tops off the tomatoes and remove all the tomato flesh and sieve into a large bowl. Sprinkle a little salt inside the tomato shells and then place them upside down on a plate while the filling is prepared.

2 Mix the sieved tomato with the breadcrumbs, fresh herbs and mushrooms and season well with salt and pepper. Place the tomato shells on the prepared baking tray and fill with the tomato and mushroom mixture. Sprinkle the cheese on the top and bake in the preheated oven for 15–20 minutes, until golden brown.

3 Meanwhile, prepare the salad. Arrange the endive and radicchio on individual serving plates and mix the remaining ingredients together in a small bowl to make the dressing. Season to taste.

4 When the tomatoes are cooked, allow to rest for 5 minutes, then place on the prepared plates and drizzle over a little dressing. Serve warm.

FOOD FACT

As an alternative, try stirring in either 2 tablespoons of tapenade or ready-made pesto into the stuffing mixture. Alternatively, replace the chives with freshly chopped basil.

CORIANDER CHICKEN OY SAUCE CAKES

INGREDIENTS   Serves 4

¼ cucumber, peeled

1 shallot, peeled and thinly sliced

6 radishes, trimmed and sliced

350 g/12 oz skinless boneless chicken thigh

4 tbsp roughly chopped fresh coriander

2 spring onions, trimmed and roughly chopped

1 red chilli, deseeded and chopped

finely grated rind of ½ lime

2 tbsp soy sauce

1 tbsp caster sugar

2 tbsp rice vinegar

1 red chilli, deseeded and finely sliced

freshly chopped coriander, to garnish

1 Preheat the oven to 190°C/ 375°F/Gas Mark 5. Halve the cucumber lengthwise, deseed and dice.

2 In a bowl mix the shallot and radishes. Chill until ready to serve with the diced cucumber.

3 Place the chicken thighs in a food processor and blend until coarsely chopped.

4 Add the coriander and spring onions to the chicken with the chilli, lime rind and soy sauce. Blend again until mixed.

5 Using slightly damp hands, shape the chicken mixture into 12 small rounds.

6 Place the rounds on a lightly oiled baking tray and bake in the preheated for 15 minutes, until golden.

7 In a small pan heat the sugar with 2 tablespoons of water until dissolved. Simmer until syrupy.

8 Remove from the heat and allow to cool a little, then stir in the vinegar and chilli slices. Pour over the cucumber and the radish and shallot salad. Garnish with the chopped coriander and serve the chicken cakes with the salad immediately.

FOOD FACT

In this recipe, the chicken cakes can be altered so that half chicken and half lean pork is used. This alters the flavour of the dish and works really well if a small 2.5 cm/ 1 inch piece of fresh ginger is grated and added in step 4.

CRISPY PRAWNS WITH CHINESE DIPPING SAUCE

INGREDIENTS   Serves 4

450 g/1 lb medium-sized raw
  prawns, peeled
¼ tsp salt
6 tbsp groundnut oil
2 garlic cloves, peeled and
  finely chopped
2.5 cm/1 inch piece fresh root
  ginger, peeled and finely
  chopped
1 green chilli, deseeded and
  finely chopped

4 stems fresh coriander, leaves
  and stems roughly chopped

**FOR THE CHINESE DIPPING
SAUCE:**
3 tbsp dark soy sauce
3 tbsp rice wine vinegar
1 tbsp caster sugar
2 tbsp chilli oil
2 spring onions, finely
  shredded

1 Using a sharp knife, remove the black vein along the back of the prawns. Sprinkle the prawns with the salt and leave to stand for 15 minutes. Pat dry on absorbent kitchen paper.

2 Heat a wok or large frying pan, add the groundnut oil and when hot, add the prawns and stir-fry in 2 batches for about 1 minute, or until they turn pink and are almost cooked. Using a slotted spoon, remove the prawns and keep warm in a low oven.

3 Drain the oil from the wok, leaving 1 tablespoon. Add the garlic, ginger and chilli and cook for about 30 seconds. Add the coriander, return the prawns and stir-fry for 1–2 minutes, or until the prawns are cooked through and the garlic is golden. Turn into a warmed serving dish.

4 For the dipping sauce, using a fork, beat together the soy sauce, rice vinegar, caster sugar and chilli oil in a small bowl. Stir in the spring onions. Serve immediately with the hot prawns.

TASTY TIP

Although you must cook raw prawns thoroughly, it is equally important not to overcook them or they will become tough and chewy and lose their delicate flavour. Stir-fry them until they are pink and opaque, constantly moving them around the pan, so that they cook evenly. They will only need cooking briefly in step 3.

POTATO PANCAKES

INGREDIENTS   Serves 6

FOR THE SAUCE:
4 tbsp crème fraîche
1 tbsp horseradish sauce
grated rind and juice of 1 lime
1 tbsp freshly snipped chives

225 g/8 oz floury potatoes,
 peeled and cut into chunks
1 small egg white
2 tbsp milk
2 tsp self-raising flour

1 tbsp freshly chopped thyme
large pinch of salt
a little vegetable oil, for frying
225 g/8 oz smoked mackerel
 fillets, skinned and roughly
 chopped
fresh herbs, to garnish

1 To make the sauce, mix together the crème fraîche, horseradish, lime rind and juice and chives. Cover and reserve.

2 Place the potatoes in a large saucepan and cover with lightly salted boiling water. Bring back to the boil, cover and simmer for 15 minutes, or until the potatoes are tender. Drain and mash until smooth. Cool for 5 minutes, then whisk in the egg white, milk, flour, thyme and salt to form a thick smooth batter. Leave to stand for 30 minutes, then stir before using.

3 Heat a little oil in a heavy-based frying pan. Add 2–3 large spoonfuls of batter to make a small pancake and cook for 1–2 minutes until golden. Flip the pancake and cook for a further minute, or until golden. Repeat with the remaining batter to make 8 pancakes.

4 Arrange the pancakes on a plate and top with the smoked mackerel. Garnish with herbs and serve immediately with spoonfuls of the reserved horseradish sauce.

HELPFUL HINT

Keep the pancakes warm as you make them by stacking on a warmed plate. Place greaseproof paper between each pancake to keep them separate and fold a clean tea towel loosely over the top. If preferred, the pancakes can be made in advance and frozen, interleaved with non-stick baking parchment. To serve, thaw, then reheat the stack of pancakes, covered in tinfoil, in a moderate oven.

HOISIN CHICKEN PANCAKES

INGREDIENTS   Serves 4

3 tbsp hoisin sauce
1 garlic clove, peeled
  and crushed
2.5 cm/1 inch piece root ginger,
  peeled and finely grated
1 tbsp soy sauce
1 tsp sesame oil
salt and freshly ground
  black pepper

4 skinless chicken thighs
½ cucumber, peeled
  (optional)
12 bought Chinese pancakes
6 spring onions, trimmed
  and cut lengthways into
  fine shreds
sweet chilli dipping sauce,
  to serve

1 Preheat the oven to 190°C/ 375°F/Gas Mark 5. In a non-metallic bowl, mix the hoisin sauce with the garlic, ginger, soy sauce, sesame oil and seasoning.

2 Add the chicken thighs and turn to coat in the mixture. Cover loosely and leave in the refrigerator to marinate for 3–4 hours, turning the chicken from time to time.

3 Remove the chicken from the marinade and place in a roasting tin. Reserve the marinade. Bake in the preheated oven for 30 minutes basting occasionally with the marinade.

4 Cut the cucumber in half lengthways and remove the seeds by running a teaspoon down the middle to scoop them out. Cut into thin batons.

5 Place the pancakes in a steamer to warm or heat according to packet instructions.

Thinly slice the hot chicken and arrange on a plate with the shredded spring onions, cucumber and pancakes.

6 Place a spoonful of the chicken in the middle of each warmed pancake and top with pieces of cucumber, spring onion, and a little dipping sauce. Roll up and serve immediately.

TASTY TIP

For those with wheat allergies or who want to make this tasty dish more substantial, stir-fry the spring onions and cucumber batons in a little groundnut oil. Add a carrot cut into batons and mix in the thinly sliced chicken and reserved marinade (as prepared in step 3). Serve with steamed rice – Thai fragrant rice is particularly good.

BEETROOT RISOTTO

INGREDIENTS

Serves 6

6 tbsp extra-virgin olive oil
1 onion, peeled and finely
  chopped
2 garlic cloves, peeled and
  finely chopped
2 tsp freshly chopped thyme
1 tsp grated lemon rind
350 g/12 oz Arborio rice
150 ml/¼ pint dry white wine
900 ml/1½ pints vegetable
  stock, heated

2 tbsp double cream
225 g/8 oz cooked beetroot,
  peeled and finely chopped
2 tbsp freshly chopped parsley
75 g/3 oz Parmesan cheese,
  freshly grated
salt and freshly ground black
  pepper
sprigs of fresh thyme,
  to garnish

1 Heat half the oil in a large heavy-based frying pan. Add the onion, garlic, thyme and lemon rind. Cook for 5 minutes, stirring frequently, until the onion is soft and transparent but not coloured. Add the rice and stir until it is well coated in the oil.

2 Add the wine, then bring to the boil and boil rapidly until the wine has almost evaporated. Reduce the heat.

3 Keeping the pan over a low heat, add a ladleful of the hot stock to the rice and cook, stirring constantly, until the stock is absorbed. Continue gradually adding the stock in this way until the rice is tender; this should take about 20 minutes. You may not need all the stock.

4 Stir in the cream, chopped beetroot, parsley and half the

grated Parmesan cheese. Season to taste with salt and pepper. Garnish with sprigs of fresh thyme and serve immediately with the remaining grated Parmesan cheese.

TASTY TIP

If you buy ready-cooked beetroot, choose small ones, which are sweeter. Make sure that they are not doused in vinegar as this would spoil the flavour of the dish. If cooking your own, try baking them instead of boiling. Leave the stems intact and gently scrub to remove any dirt. Put them in a baking dish, cover loosely with tinfoil and cook in a preheated oven at 170°C/325°F/Gas Mark 3 for 2 hours. Once cool enough to handle, the skins should slip off.

AUBERGINE DIP WITH PITTA STRIPS

INGREDIENTS — Serves 4

4 pitta breads
2 large aubergines
1 garlic clove, peeled
¼ tsp sesame oil
1 tbsp lemon juice

½ tsp ground cumin
salt and freshly ground
 black pepper
2 tbsp freshly chopped parsley
fresh salad leaves, to serve

1 Preheat the oven to 180°C/ 350°F/Gas Mark 4. On a chopping board cut the pitta breads into strips. Spread the bread in a single layer on to a large baking tray.

2 Cook in the preheated oven for 15 minutes until golden and crisp. Leave to cool on a wire cooling rack.

3 Trim the aubergines, rinse lightly and reserve. Heat a griddle pan until almost smoking. Cook the aubergines and garlic for about 15 minutes.

4 Turn the aubergines frequently, until very tender with wrinkled and charred skins. Remove from heat. Leave to cool.

5 When the aubergines are cool enough to handle, cut in half and scoop out the cooked flesh and place in a food processor.

6 Squeeze the softened garlic flesh from the papery skin and add to the aubergine.

7 Blend the aubergine and garlic until smooth, then add the sesame oil, lemon juice and cumin and blend again to mix.

8 Season to taste with salt and pepper, stir in the parsley and serve with the pitta strips and mixed salad leaves.

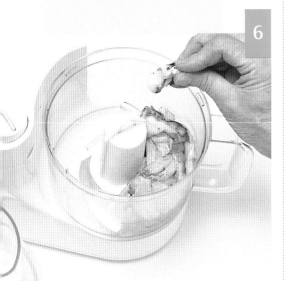

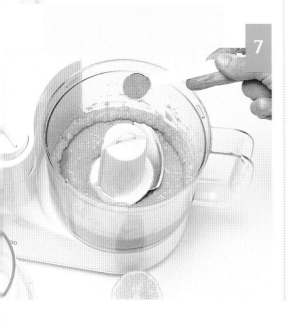

FOOD FACT

This dish is a variation on the traditional Arabic dish known as *Baba Ganoush*, which translates to "spoilt old man". As well as being great with pitta strips or bread sticks, this dish is fantastic warmed through and served as a meal accompaniment.

SMOKED SALMON WITH BROAD BEANS & RICE

INGREDIENTS   Serves 4

2 tbsp sunflower oil

25 g/1 oz unsalted butter

1 onion, peeled and chopped

2 garlic cloves, peeled and chopped

175 g/6 oz asparagus tips, halved

75 g/3 oz frozen broad beans

150 ml/¼ pint dry white wine

125 g/4 oz sun-dried tomatoes, drained and sliced

125 g/4 oz baby spinach leaves, washed

450 g/1 lb cooked long-grain rice

3 tbsp crème fraîche

225 g/8 oz smoked salmon, cut into strips

75 g/3 oz freshly grated Parmesan cheese

salt and freshly ground black pepper

1 Heat a large wok, then add the oil and butter and, when melted, stir-fry the onion for 3 minutes, until almost softened. Add the garlic and asparagus tips and stir-fry for 3 minutes. Add the broad beans and wine and bring to the boil, then simmer, stirring occasionally, until the wine is reduced slightly.

2 Add the sun-dried tomatoes and bring back to the boil, then simmer for 2 minutes. Stir in the baby spinach leaves and cooked rice and return to the boil. Stir-fry for 2 minutes, or until the spinach is wilted and the rice is heated through thoroughly.

3 Stir in the crème fraîche, smoked salmon strips and Parmesan cheese. Stir well and cook, stirring frequently, until piping hot. Season to taste with salt and pepper. Serve immediately.

HELPFUL HINT

To make 450 g/1 lb cooked rice, measure 175 g/6 oz long-grain rice. Wash well in several changes of water and drain. Put into a saucepan with enough cold water to cover the rice by about 2.5 cm/ 1 inch, add salt and stir well. Bring to the boil over a high heat, then reduce the heat to very low, cover and cook for 10 minutes. Remove from the heat and leave, covered, for a further 10 minutes. Do not lift the lid until the full 20 minutes have elapsed.

BARBECUED FISH KEBABS

3

INGREDIENTS   Serves 4

450 g/1 lb herring
  or mackerel fillets, cut
  into chunks
2 small red onions, peeled
  and quartered
16 cherry tomatoes
salt and freshly ground
  black pepper

FOR THE SAUCE:
150 ml /¼ pint fish stock
5 tbsp tomato ketchup
2 tbsp Worcestershire sauce
2 tbsp wine vinegar
2 tbsp brown sugar
2 drops Tabasco
2 tbsp tomato purée

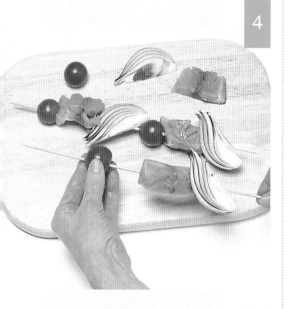

4

1 Line a grill rack with a single layer of tinfoil and preheat the grill at a high temperature, 2 minutes before use.

2 If using wooden skewers, soak in cold water for 30 minutes to prevent them from catching alight during cooking.

3 Meanwhile, prepare the sauce. Add the fish stock, tomato ketchup, Worcestershire sauce, vinegar, sugar, Tabasco and tomato purée to a small saucepan. Stir well and leave to simmer for 5 minutes.

5

4 When ready to cook, drain the skewers, if necessary, then thread the fish chunks, the quartered red onions and the cherry tomatoes alternately on to the skewers.

5 Season the kebabs to taste with salt and pepper and brush with the sauce. Grill under the preheated grill for 8–10 minutes, basting with the sauce occasionally during cooking. Turn the kebabs often to ensure that they are cooked thoroughly and evenly on all sides. Serve immediately with couscous.

TASTY TIP

This dish would be ideal for a light summertime evening meal. Instead of cooking indoors, cook these kebabs on the barbecue for a delicious charcoaled flavour. Light the barbecue at least 20 minutes before use in order to allow the coals to heat up. (The coals will have a grey-white ash when ready.) Barbecue some peppers and red onions and serve with a mixed salad as an accompaniment to the fish kebabs.

SALMON WITH STRAWBERRY SAUCE

INGREDIENTS   Serves 4

4 x 150 g/5 oz salmon fillets
25 g/1 oz butter
2 tbsp groundnut oil
1 dessert apple, cored and cut into chunks
1 bunch spring onions, trimmed and diagonally sliced
1 garlic clove, peeled and sliced
50 g/2 oz pine nuts

juice of 1 lemon
125 g/4 oz strawberries, hulled and halved
1 bunch basil, freshly chopped
salt and freshly ground black pepper

TO SERVE:
freshly cooked creamy mashed potatoes
freshly cooked broad beans

1 Wash the salmon fillets and pat dry on absorbent kitchen paper. Heat the wok, then add the butter and half the oil and heat until bubbling. Cook the salmon fillets flesh side down for 5 minutes, until they are sealed. Then, using a fish slice, carefully turn the salmon fillets over and cook for a further 3–5 minutes, until the salmon flesh is just flaking.

2 Transfer the salmon fillets to warmed serving plates and keep warm in a low oven. Wipe the wok clean, then add the remaining oil to the wok and heat until almost smoking.

3 Add the apple chunks, spring onions, garlic slices and pine nuts and cook for 5 minutes, stirring occasionally, until they are golden brown.

4 Stir in the lemon juice, strawberries, chopped basil and season to taste with salt and pepper. Heat through thoroughly.

5 Spoon the sauce over the salmon fillets and serve immediately with creamy mashed potatoes and freshly cooked broad beans.

HELPFUL HINT

This unusual fruit sauce provides a much-needed sharpness against the richness of the fish. Do not overcook the strawberries, however, or they will lose their shape and texture.

SALMON FISH CAKES

INGREDIENTS

Serves 4

450 g/1 lb salmon fillet, skinned

salt and freshly ground black pepper

450 g/1 lb potatoes, peeled and cut into chunks

25 g/1 oz butter

1 tbsp milk

2 medium tomatoes, skinned, deseeded and chopped

2 tbsp freshly chopped parsley

75 g/3 oz wholemeal breadcrumbs

25 g/1 oz Cheddar cheese, grated

2 tbsp plain flour

2 medium eggs, beaten

3–4 tbsp vegetable oil

TO SERVE:

ready-made raita

sprigs of fresh mint

1 Place the salmon in a shallow frying pan and cover with water. Season to taste with salt and pepper and simmer for 8–10 minutes until the fish is cooked. Drain and flake into a bowl.

2 Boil the potatoes in lightly salted water until soft, then drain. Mash with the butter and milk until smooth. Add the potato to the bowl of fish and stir in the tomatoes and half the parsley. Adjust the seasoning to taste. Chill the mixture in the refrigerator for at least 2 hours to firm up.

3 Mix the breadcrumbs with the grated cheese and the remaining parsley. When the fish mixture is firm, form into 8 flat cakes. First, lightly coat the fish cakes in the flour, then dip into the beaten egg, allowing any excess to drip back into the bowl. Finally, press into the breadcrumb mixture until well coated.

4 Heat a little of the oil in a frying pan and fry the fish cakes in batches for 2–3 minutes on each side until golden and crisp, adding more oil if necessary. Serve with raita garnished with sprigs of mint.

HELPFUL HINT

To remove the skins from the tomatoes, pierce each with the tip of a sharp knife, then plunge into boiling water and leave for up to 1 minute. Drain, then rinse in cold water – the skins should peel off easily. Alternatively, hold them over a gas flame with a fork for a few seconds, turning until the skin is slightly blackened and blistered.

SALMON NOISETTES WITH FRUITY SAUCE

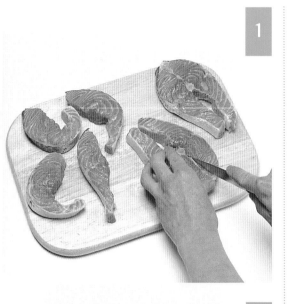

INGREDIENTS — Serves 4

4 x 125 g/4 oz salmon steaks
grated rind and juice of 2
 lemons
grated rind and juice of
 1 lime
3 tbsp olive oil
1 tbsp clear honey
1 tbsp wholegrain mustard
coarse sea salt and freshly
 ground black pepper
1 tbsp groundnut oil

125 g/4 oz mixed salad leaves,
 washed
1 bunch watercress, washed
 and thick stalks removed
250 g/9 oz baby plum
 tomatoes, halved

1 Using a sharp knife, cut the bone away from each salmon steak to create 2 salmon fillets. Repeat with the remaining salmon steaks. Shape the salmon fillets into noisettes and secure with fine string.

2 Mix together the citrus rinds and juices, olive oil, honey, wholegrain mustard, salt and pepper in a shallow dish. Add the salmon fillets and turn to coat. Cover and leave to marinate in the refrigerator for 4 hours, turning them occasionally in the marinade.

3 Heat the wok then add the groundnut oil and heat until hot. Lift out the salmon noisettes, reserving the marinade. Add the salmon to the wok and cook for 6–10 minutes, turning once during cooking, until cooked and the fish is just flaking. Pour the marinade into the wok and heat through gently.

4 Mix together the salad leaves, watercress and tomatoes and arrange on serving plates. Top with the salmon noisettes and drizzle over any remaining warm marinade. Serve immediately.

HELPFUL HINT

When choosing salad leaves for this dish, look out for slightly bitter leaves such as frisée and radicchio, which will stand up well to the heat of the salmon and contrast well with the sweetness of the sauce.

COD WITH FENNEL & CARDAMOM

INGREDIENTS   Serves 4

1 garlic clove, peeled
  and crushed
finely grated rind of 1 lemon
1 tsp lemon juice
1 tbsp olive oil

1 fennel bulb
1 tbsp cardamom pods
salt and freshly ground
  black pepper
4 x 175 g/6 oz thick cod fillets

1 Preheat the oven to 190°C/ 375°F/Gas Mark 5. Place the garlic in a small bowl with the lemon rind, juice and olive oil and stir well.

2 Cover and leave to infuse for at least 30 minutes. Stir well before using.

3 Trim the fennel bulb, thinly slice and place in a bowl.

4 Place the cardamom pods in a pestle and mortar and lightly pound to crack the pods.

5 Alternatively place in a polythene bag and pound gently with a rolling pin. Add the crushed cardamom to the fennel slices.

6 Season the fish with salt and pepper and place on to 4 separate 20.5 x 20.5 cm /8 x 8 inch parchment paper squares.

7 Spoon the fennel mixture over the fish and drizzle with the infused oil.

8 Place the parcels on a baking sheet and bake in the preheated oven for 8–10 minutes or until cooked. Serve immediately in the paper parcels.

FOOD FACT

When buying fresh fish, look for fish that does not smell. Any ammonia-type smelling fish should be avoided. The flesh should be plump and firm-looking. The eyes should be bright, not sunken. If in doubt, choose frozen fish. This is cleaned and packed almost as soon as it is caught. It is often fresher and contains more nutrients than its fresh counterparts.

SPICY COD RICE

INGREDIENTS   Serves 4

1 tbsp plain flour
1 tbsp freshly chopped
  coriander
1 tsp ground cumin
1 tsp ground coriander
550 g/1¼ lb thick-cut cod fillet,
  skinned and cut into large
  chunks
4 tbsp groundnut oil
50 g/2 oz cashew nuts
1 bunch spring onions,
  trimmed and diagonally
  sliced

1 red chilli, deseeded and
  chopped
1 carrot, peeled and cut into
  matchsticks
125 g/4 oz frozen peas
450 g/1 lb cooked long-grain
  rice
2 tbsp sweet chilli sauce
2 tbsp soy sauce

1 Mix together the flour, coriander, cumin and ground coriander on a large plate. Coat the cod in the spice mixture then place on a baking sheet, cover and chill in the refrigerator for 30 minutes.

2 Heat a large wok, then add 2 tablespoons of the oil and heat until almost smoking. Stir-fry the cashew nuts for 1 minute, until browned, then remove and reserve.

3 Add a further 1 tablespoon of the oil and heat until almost smoking. Add the cod and stir-fry for 2 minutes. Using a fish slice, turn the cod pieces over and cook for a further 2 minutes, until golden. Remove from the wok, place on a warm plate, cover and keep warm.

4 Add the remaining oil to the wok, heat until almost smoking then stir-fry the spring onions and chilli for 1 minute before adding the carrots and peas and stir-frying for a further 2 minutes. Stir in the rice, chilli sauce, soy sauce and cashew nuts and stir-fry for 3 more minutes. Add the cod, heat for 1 minute, then serve immediately.

HELPFUL HINT

Care is needed when frying nuts as they have a tendency to turn from golden to burnt very quickly. An alternative is to toast them on a baking sheet in the oven at 180°C/350°F/Gas Mark 4 for about 5 minutes until they are golden and fragrant.

CHUNKY HALIBUT CASSEROLE

INGREDIENTS   Serves 6

50 g/2 oz butter or margarine
2 large onions, peeled and
   sliced into rings
1 red pepper, deseeded and
   roughly chopped
450 g/1 lb potatoes, peeled
450 g/1 lb courgettes, trimmed
   and thickly sliced
2 tbsp plain flour
1 tbsp paprika
2 tsp vegetable oil

300 ml/½ pint white wine
150 ml/¼ pint fish stock
400 g can chopped tomatoes
2 tbsp freshly chopped basil
salt and freshly ground black
   pepper
450 g/1 lb halibut fillet,
   skinned and cut into 2.5 cm/
   1 inch cubes
sprigs of fresh basil, to garnish
freshly cooked rice, to serve

1 Melt the butter or margarine in a large saucepan, add the onions and pepper and cook for 5 minutes, or until softened.

2 Cut the peeled potatoes into 2.5 cm/1 inch dice, rinse lightly and shake dry, then add them to the onions and pepper in the saucepan. Add the courgettes and cook, stirring frequently, for a further 2–3 minutes.

3 Sprinkle the flour, paprika and vegetable oil into the saucepan and cook, stirring continuously, for 1 minute. Pour in 150 ml/¼ pint of the wine, with all the stock and the chopped tomatoes, and bring to the boil.

4 Add the basil to the casserole, season to taste with salt and pepper and cover. Simmer for 15 minutes, then add the halibut and the remaining wine and

simmer very gently for a further 5–7 minutes, or until the fish and vegetables are just tender. Garnish with basil sprigs and serve immediately with freshly cooked rice.

FOOD FACT

Halibut is a flatfish with firm, milky white flesh that has an almost meaty texture, making it ideal for this casserole. They can grow to an enormous size, at times weighing in at over 200 kg/ 444 lb, and are fished in the deep, freezing-cold waters of the North Sea.

CHINESE STEAMED SEA BASS WITH BLACK BEANS

INGREDIENTS   Serves 4

1.1 kg/2½ lb sea bass, cleaned with head and tail left on

1–2 tbsp rice wine or dry sherry

1½ tbsp groundnut oil

2–3 tbsp fermented black beans, rinsed and drained

1 garlic clove, peeled and finely chopped

1 cm/½ inch piece fresh root ginger, peeled and finely chopped

4 spring onions, trimmed and thinly sliced diagonally

2–3 tbsp soy sauce

125 ml/4 fl oz fish or chicken stock

1–2 tbsp sweet Chinese chilli sauce, or to taste

2 tsp sesame oil

sprigs of fresh coriander, to garnish

1 Using a sharp knife, cut 3–4 deep diagonal slashes along both sides of the fish. Sprinkle the Chinese rice wine or sherry inside and over the fish and gently rub into the skin on both sides.

2 Lightly brush a heatproof plate large enough to fit into a large wok or frying pan with a little of the groundnut oil. Place the fish on the plate, curving the fish along the inside edge of the dish, then leave for 20 minutes.

3 Place a wire rack or inverted ramekin in the wok and pour in enough water to come about 2.5 cm/1 inch up the side. Bring to the boil over a high heat.

4 Carefully place the plate with the fish on the rack or ramekin, cover and steam for 12–15 minutes, or until the fish is tender and the flesh is opaque when pierced with a knife near the bone.

5 Remove the plate with the fish from the wok and keep warm. Remove the rack or ramekin from the wok and pour off the water. Return the wok to the heat, add the remaining groundnut oil and swirl to coat the bottom and side. Add the black beans, garlic and ginger and stir-fry for 1 minute.

6 Add the spring onions, soy sauce, fish or chicken stock and boil for 1 minute. Stir in the chilli sauce and sesame oil, then pour the sauce over the cooked fish. Garnish with coriander sprigs and serve immediately.

POTATO BOULANGERE WITH SEA BASS

INGREDIENTS   Serves 2

450 g/1 lb potatoes, peeled and thinly sliced
1 large onion, peeled and thinly sliced
salt and freshly ground black pepper

300 ml/½ pint fish or vegetable stock
75 g/3 oz butter or margarine
350 g/12 oz sea bass fillets
sprigs of fresh flat-leaf parsley, to garnish

1 Preheat the oven to 200°C/400°F/Gas Mark 6. Lightly grease a shallow 1.4 litre/2½ pint baking dish with oil or butter. Layer the potato slices and onions alternately in the prepared dish, seasoning each layer with salt and pepper.

2 Pour the stock over the top, then cut 50 g/2 oz of the butter or margarine into small pieces and dot over the top layer. Bake in the preheated oven for 50–60 minutes. Do not cover the dish at this stage.

3 Lightly rinse the sea bass fillets and pat dry on absorbent kitchen paper. Cook in a griddle, or heat the remaining butter or margarine in a frying pan and shallow fry the fish fillets for 3–4 minutes per side, flesh side first. Remove from the pan with a slotted spatula and drain on absorbent kitchen paper.

4 Remove the partly cooked potato and onion mixture from the oven and place the fish on the top. Cover with tinfoil and return to the oven for 10 minutes until heated through. Garnish with sprigs of parsley and serve immediately.

FOOD FACT

Sea bass, also known as sea perch, is a large round fish which grows up to 1 m/3⅓ ft long, and may weigh up to 9 kg/20 lb. In appearance, it is similar to a salmon, but a much darker grey colour. Cook it gently and handle it with care, as the flesh is soft and delicate.

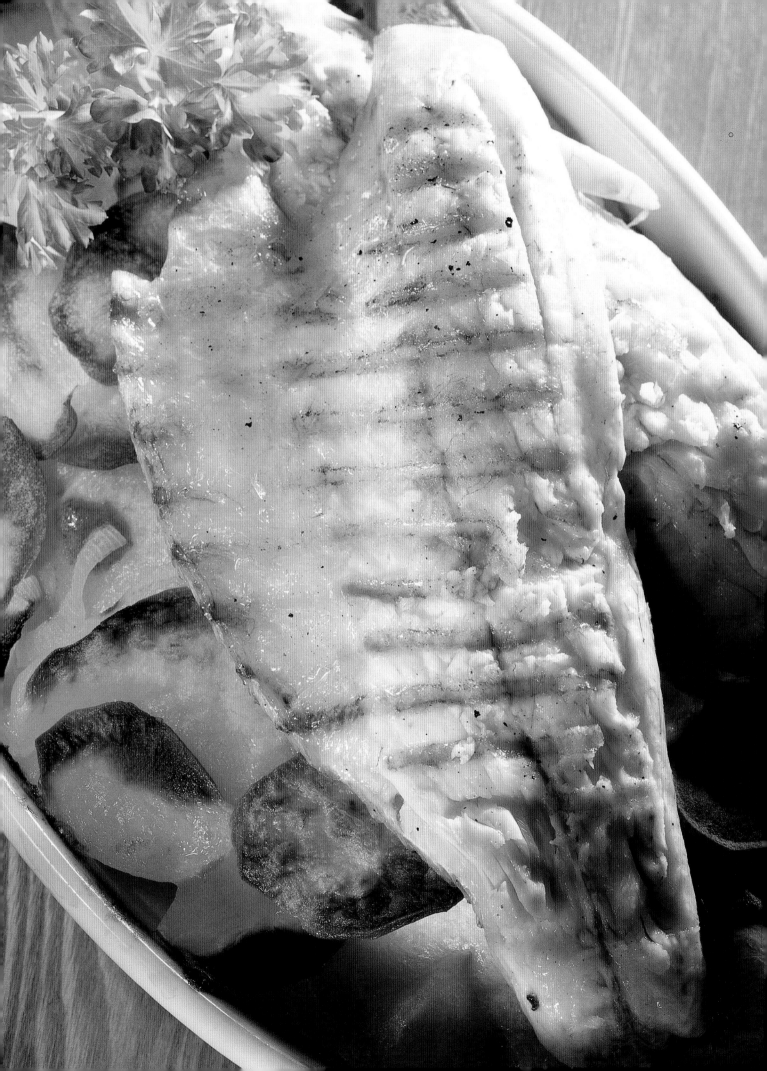

Pasta Provençale

INGREDIENTS   Serves 4

2 tbsp olive oil
1 garlic clove, peeled and crushed
1 onion, peeled and finely chopped
1 small fennel bulb, trimmed and halved and thinly sliced
400 g can chopped tomatoes
1 rosemary sprig, plus extra sprig to garnish
350 g/12 oz monkfish, skinned

2 tsp lemon juice
400 g/14 oz gnocchi pasta
50 g/2 oz pitted black olives
200 g can flageolet beans, drained and rinsed
1 tbsp freshly chopped oregano, plus sprig to garnish
salt and freshly ground black pepper

1 Heat the olive oil in a large saucepan, add the garlic and onion and cook gently for 5 minutes. Add the fennel and cook for a further 5 minutes. Stir in the chopped tomatoes and rosemary sprig. Half-cover the pan and simmer for 10 minutes.

2 Cut the monkfish into bite-sized pieces and sprinkle with the lemon juice. Add to the tomatoes, cover and simmer gently for 5 minutes, or until the fish is opaque.

3 Meanwhile, bring a large pan of lightly salted water to a rolling boil. Add the pasta and cook according to the packet instructions, or until 'al dente'. Drain the pasta thoroughly and return to the saucepan.

4 Remove the rosemary from the tomato sauce. Stir in the black olives, flageolet beans and chopped oregano, then season to taste with salt and pepper. Add the sauce to the pasta and toss gently together to coat, taking care not to break up the monkfish. Tip into a warmed serving bowl. Garnish with rosemary and oregano sprigs and serve immediately.

FOOD FACT

Only the tail of the monkfish is eaten and this is usually sold skinned. It has a firm, very white, almost meaty flesh and just one bone running down the middle. It may still have a tough transparent membrane covering it, which should be carefully removed before cooking. A less expensive firm white fish, such as haddock, may be used if preferred.

GRILLED RED MULLET WITH ORANGE & ANCHOVY SAUCE

INGREDIENTS   Serves 4

2 oranges
4 x 175 g/6 oz red mullet,
  cleaned and descaled
salt and freshly ground black
  pepper
4 sprigs of fresh rosemary
1 lemon, sliced
2 tbsp olive oil

2 garlic cloves, peeled and
  crushed
6 anchovies fillets in oil,
  drained and roughly
  chopped
2 tsp freshly chopped
  rosemary
1 tsp lemon juice

1 Preheat the grill and line the grill rack with tinfoil just before cooking. Peel the oranges with a sharp knife, over a bowl in order to catch the juice. Cut into thin slices and reserve. If necessary, make up the juice to 150 ml/¼ pint with extra juice.

2 Place the fish on a chopping board and make 2 diagonal slashes across the thickest part of both sides of the fish. Season well, both inside and out, with salt and pepper. Tuck a rosemary sprig and a few lemon slices inside the cavity of each fish. Brush the fish with a little of the olive oil and then cook under the preheated grill for 4–5 minutes on each side. The flesh should just fall away from the bone.

3 Heat the remaining oil in a saucepan and gently fry the garlic and anchovies for 3–4 minutes. Do not allow to brown.

Add the chopped rosemary and plenty of black pepper. The anchovies will be salty enough, so do not add any salt. Stir in the orange slices with their juice and the lemon juice. Simmer gently until heated through. Spoon the sauce over the red mullet and serve immediately.

FOOD FACT

Red mullet is a fairly common fish but size can vary enormously – often only very large fish are available. Substitute with grey mullet or snapper, if necessary.

SEARED TUNA WITH PERNOD & THYME

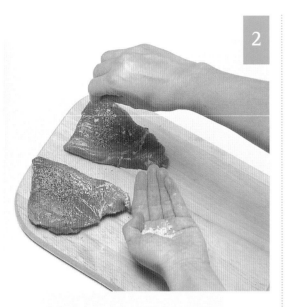

INGREDIENTS   Serves 4

4 tuna or swordfish steaks
salt and freshly ground
    black pepper
3 tbsp Pernod
1 tbsp olive oil
zest and juice of 1 lime

2 tsp fresh thyme leaves
4 sun-dried tomatoes

TO SERVE:
freshly cooked mixed rice
tossed green salad

1 Wipe the fish steaks with a damp cloth or dampened kitchen paper.

2 Season both sides of the fish to taste with salt and pepper, then place in a shallow bowl and reserve.

3 Mix together the Pernod, olive oil, lime zest and juice with the fresh thyme leaves.

4 Finely chop the sun-dried tomatoes and add to the Pernod mixture.

5 Pour the Pernod mixture over the fish and chill in the refrigerator for about 2 hours, spooning the marinade occasionally over the fish.

6 Heat a griddle or heavy-based frying pan. Drain the fish, reserving the marinade. Cook the fish for 3–4 minutes on each side for a steak that is still slightly pink in the middle. Or, if liked, cook the fish for

1–2 minutes longer on each side if you prefer your fish cooked through.

7 Place the remaining marinade in a small saucepan and bring to the boil. Pour the marinade over the fish and serve immediately, with the mixed rice and salad.

HELPFUL HINT

Tuna is now widely available all year round at fishmongers and in supermarkets. Tuna is an oily fish rich in Omega-3 fatty acids which help in the prevention of heart disease by lowering blood cholesterol levels. Tuna is usually sold in steaks, and the flesh should be dark red in colour.

TUNA & MUSHROOM RAGOUT

INGREDIENTS   Serves 4

225 g/8 oz basmati and wild rice
50 g/2 oz butter
1 tbsp olive oil
1 large onion, peeled and finely chopped
1 garlic clove, peeled and crushed
300 g/11 oz baby button mushrooms, wiped and halved
2 tbsp plain flour
400 g can chopped tomatoes

1 tbsp freshly chopped parsley
dash of Worcestershire sauce
400 g can tuna in oil, drained
salt and freshly ground black pepper
4 tbsp Parmesan cheese, grated
1 tbsp freshly shredded basil

TO SERVE:
green salad
garlic bread

1 Cook the basmati and wild rice in a saucepan of boiling salted water for 20 minutes, then drain and return to the pan. Stir in half of the butter, cover the pan and leave to stand for 2 minutes until all of the butter has melted.

2 Heat the oil and the remaining butter in a frying pan and cook the onion for 1–2 minutes until soft. Add the garlic and mushrooms and continue to cook for a further 3 minutes.

3 Stir in the flour and cook for 1 minute, then add the tomatoes and bring the sauce to the boil. Add the parsley, Worcestershire sauce and tuna and simmer gently for 3 minutes. Season to taste with salt and freshly ground pepper.

4 Stir the rice well, then spoon onto 4 serving plates and top with the tuna and mushroom mixture. Sprinkle with a spoonful of grated Parmesan cheese and some shredded basil for each portion and serve immediately with a green salad and chunks of garlic bread.

TASTY TIP

Fresh basil adds a wonderful flavour and fragrance to this dish, but sometimes it can be difficult to find during the winter months. If you have problems finding it, buy chopped tomatoes that have basil already added to them, or use extra freshly chopped parsley instead.

FRESH TUNA SALAD

INGREDIENTS
Serves 4

225 g/8 oz mixed salad leaves
225 g/8 oz baby cherry
tomatoes, halved
lengthways
125 g/4 oz rocket leaves,
washed
2 tbsp groundnut oil
550 g/1¼ lb boned tuna steaks,
each cut into 4 small pieces

50 g/2 oz piece fresh
Parmesan cheese

FOR THE DRESSING:
8 tbsp olive oil
grated zest and juice of
2 small lemons
1 tbsp wholegrain mustard
salt and freshly ground
black pepper

1 Wash the salad leaves and place in a large salad bowl with the cherry tomatoes and rocket and reserve.

2 Heat the wok, then add the oil and heat until almost smoking. Add the tuna, skin-side down, and cook for 4–6 minutes, turning once during cooking, or until cooked and the flesh flakes easily. Remove from the heat and leave to stand in the juices for 2 minutes before removing.

3 Meanwhile make the dressing, place the olive oil, lemon zest and juices and mustard in a small bowl or screw-topped jar and whisk or shake well until well blended. Season to taste with salt and pepper.

4 Transfer the tuna to a clean chopping board and flake, then add it to the salad and toss lightly.

5 Using a swivel blade vegetable peeler, peel the piece of Parmesan cheese into shavings. Divide the salad between 4 large serving plates, drizzle the dressing over the salad, then scatter with the Parmesan shavings.

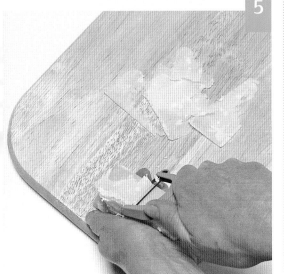
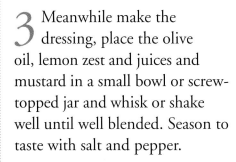

HELPFUL HINT

Bags of mixed salad leaves are available from all major supermarkets. Although they seem expensive, there is very little waste and they do save time. Rinse the leaves before using.

Tagliatelle with Tuna & Anchovy Tapenade

INGREDIENTS Serves 4

400 g/14 oz tagliatelle
125 g can tuna fish in oil, drained
45 g/1¾ oz can anchovy fillets, drained
150 g/5 oz pitted black olives
2 tbsp capers in brine, drained

2 tsp lemon juice
100 ml/3½ fl oz olive oil
2 tbsp freshly chopped parsley
freshly ground black pepper
sprigs of flat-leaf parsley, to garnish

1 Bring a large pan of lightly salted water to a rolling boil. Add the tagliatelle and cook according to the packet instructions, or until 'al dente'.

2 Meanwhile, place the tuna fish, anchovy fillets, olives and capers in a food processor with the lemon juice and 2 tablespoons of the olive oil and blend for a few seconds until roughly chopped.

3 With the motor running, pour in the remaining olive oil in a steady stream; the resulting mixture should be slightly chunky rather than smooth.

4 Spoon the sauce into a bowl, stir in the chopped parsley and season to taste with black pepper. Check the taste of the sauce and add a little more lemon juice, if required.

5 Drain the pasta thoroughly. Pour the sauce into the pan and cook over a low heat for 1–2 minutes to warm through.

6 Return the drained pasta to the pan and mix together with the sauce. Tip into a warmed serving bowl or spoon on to warm individual plates. Garnish with sprigs of flat-leaf parsley and serve immediately.

HELPFUL HINT

Capers are the flower buds of the caper bush, which grows throughout the Mediterranean region. The buds are picked before they open and preserved in vinegar and salt. The word tapenade (a mixture of capers, olives and fish, usually anchovies, pounded to a paste with olive oil) comes from the Provençal word for capers – tapeno.

SARDINES WITH REDCURRANTS

INGREDIENTS   Serves 4

2 tbsp redcurrant jelly
finely grated rind of 1 lime
2 tbsp medium dry sherry
450 g /1 lb fresh sardines,
   cleaned and heads removed
sea salt and freshly ground
   black pepper
lime wedges, to garnish

TO SERVE:
fresh redcurrants
fresh green salad

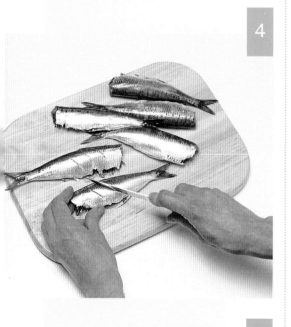

1 Preheat the grill and line the grill rack with tinfoil 2–3 minutes before cooking.

2 Warm the redcurrant jelly in a bowl standing over a pan of gently simmering water and stir until smooth. Add the lime rind and sherry to the bowl and stir well until blended.

3 Lightly rinse the sardines and pat dry with absorbent kitchen paper.

4 Place on a chopping board and with a sharp knife make several diagonal cuts across the flesh of each fish. Season the sardines inside the cavities with salt and pepper.

5 Gently brush the warm marinade over the skin and inside the cavities of the sardines.

6 Place on the grill rack and cook under the preheated grill for 8–10 minutes, or until the fish are cooked.

7 Carefully turn the sardines over at least once during grilling. Baste occasionally with the remaining redcurrant and lime marinade. Garnish with the redcurrants. Serve immediately with the salad and lime wedges.

COOK'S TIP

Most fish are sold cleaned but it is easy to do yourself. Using the back of a knife, scrape off the scales from the tail towards the head. Make a small slit along their bellies using a sharp knife. Carefully scrape out the entrails and rinse thoroughly under cold running water. Pat dry with absorbent paper.

FRAGRANT THAI SWORDFISH WITH PEPPERS

INGREDIENTS   Serves 4–6

550 g/1¼ lb swordfish, cut into 5 cm/2 inch strips
2 tbsp vegetable oil
2 lemon grass stalks, peeled, bruised and cut into 2.5 cm/ 1 inch pieces
2.5 cm/1 inch piece fresh root ginger, peeled and thinly sliced
4–5 shallots, peeled and thinly sliced
2–3 garlic cloves, peeled and thinly sliced
1 small red pepper, deseeded and thinly sliced
1 small yellow pepper, deseeded and thinly sliced

2 tbsp soy sauce
2 tbsp Chinese rice wine or dry sherry
1–2 tsp sugar
1 tsp sesame oil
1 tbsp Thai or Italian basil, shredded
salt and freshly ground black pepper
1 tbsp toasted sesame seeds

FOR THE MARINADE:
1 tbsp soy sauce
1 tbsp Chinese rice wine or dry sherry
1 tbsp sesame oil
1 tbsp cornflour

1 Blend all the marinade ingredients together in a shallow, nonmetallic baking dish. Add the swordfish and spoon the marinade over the fish. Cover and leave to marinate in the refrigerator for at least 30 minutes.

2 Using a slotted spatula or spoon, remove the swordfish from the marinade and drain briefly on absorbent kitchen paper. Heat a wok or large frying pan, add the oil and when hot, add the swordfish and stir-fry for 2 minutes, or until it begins to brown. Remove the swordfish and drain on absorbent kitchen paper.

3 Add the lemon grass, ginger, shallots and garlic to the wok and stir-fry for 30 seconds. Add the peppers, soy sauce, Chinese rice wine or sherry and sugar and stir-fry for 3–4 minutes.

4 Return the swordfish to the wok and stir-fry gently for 1–2 minutes, or until heated through and coated with the sauce. If necessary, moisten the sauce with a little of the marinade or some water. Stir in the sesame oil and the basil and season to taste with salt and pepper. Tip into a warmed serving bowl, sprinkle with sesame seeds and serve immediately.

Scallops & Monkfish Kebabs with Fennel Sauce

INGREDIENTS   Serves 4

700 g/1½ lb monkfish tail
8 large fresh scallops
2 tbsp olive oil
1 garlic clove, peeled and
 crushed
freshly ground black pepper
1 fennel bulb, trimmed and
 thinly sliced
assorted salad leaves, to serve

FOR THE SAUCE:
2 tbsp fennel seeds
pinch of chilli flakes
4 tbsp olive oil
2 tsp lemon juice
salt and freshly ground black
 pepper

1 Place the monkfish on a chopping board and remove the skin and the bone that runs down the centre of the tail and discard. Lightly rinse and pat dry with absorbent kitchen paper. Cut the 2 fillets into 12 equal-sized pieces and place in a shallow bowl.

2 Remove the scallops from their shells, if necessary, and clean thoroughly discarding the black vein. Rinse lightly and pat dry with absorbent kitchen paper. Put in the bowl with the fish.

3 Blend the 2 tablespoons of olive oil, the crushed garlic and a pinch of black pepper in a small bowl, then pour the mixture over the monkfish and scallops, making sure they are well coated. Cover lightly and leave to marinate in the refrigerator for at least 30 minutes, or longer if time permits. Spoon over the marinade occasionally.

4 Lightly crush the fennel seeds and chilli flakes in a pestle and mortar. Stir in the 4 tablespoons of olive oil and lemon juice and season to taste with salt and pepper. Cover and leave to infuse for 20 minutes.

5 Drain the monkfish and scallops, reserving the marinade and thread on to 4 skewers.

6 Spray a griddle pan with a fine spray of oil, then heat until almost smoking and cook the kebabs for 5–6 minutes, turning halfway through and brushing with the marinade throughout.

7 Brush the fennel slices with the fennel sauce and cook on the griddle for 1 minute on each side. Serve the fennel slices, topped with the kebabs and drizzled with the fennel sauce. Serve with a few assorted salad leaves.

FISH ROULADES WITH RICE & SPINACH

INGREDIENTS — Serves 4

4 x 175 g/6 oz lemon sole, skinned
salt and freshly ground black pepper
1 tsp fennel seeds
75 g/3 oz long-grain rice, cooked
150 g/5 oz white crab meat, fresh or canned

125 g/4 oz baby spinach, washed and trimmed
5 tbsp dry white wine
5 tbsp half-fat crème fraîche
2 tbsp freshly chopped parsley, plus extra to garnish
asparagus spears, to serve

1 Wipe each fish fillet with either a clean damp cloth or kitchen paper. Place on a chopping board, skinned side up and season lightly with salt and black pepper.

2 Place the fennel seeds in a pestle and mortar and crush lightly. Transfer to a small bowl and stir in the cooked rice. Drain the crab meat thoroughly. Add to the rice mixture and mix lightly.

3 Lay 2–3 spinach leaves over each fillet and top with a quarter of the crab meat mixture. Roll up and secure with a cocktail stick if necessary. Place into a large pan and pour over the wine. Cover and cook on a medium heat for 5–7 minutes or until cooked.

4 Remove the fish from the cooking liquor, and transfer to a serving plate and keep warm. Stir the crème fraîche into the cooking liquor and season to taste. Heat for 3 minutes, then stir in the chopped parsley.

5 Spoon the sauce on to the base of a plate. Cut each roulade into slices and arrange on top of the sauce. Serve with freshly cooked asparagus spears.

FOOD FACT

Spinach is one of the healthiest, leafy green vegetables to be eaten. It also acts as an antioxidant and it is suggested that it can reduce risks of certain cancers. Why not use whole-grain rice to add nutritional value and to give the dish a nuttier taste.

LAMB PILAF

INGREDIENTS   Serves 4

2 tbsp vegetable oil
25 g/1 oz flaked or slivered
    almonds
1 medium onion, peeled and
    finely chopped
1 medium carrot, peeled and
    finely chopped
1 celery stalk, trimmed and
    finely chopped
350 g/12 oz lean lamb, cut into
    chunks
¼ tsp ground cinnamon
¼ tsp chilli flakes
2 large tomatoes, skinned,
    deseeded and chopped

grated rind of 1 orange
350 g/12 oz easy-cook brown
    basmati rice
600 ml/1 pint vegetable or
    lamb stock
2 tbsp freshly snipped chives
3 tbsp freshly chopped
    coriander
salt and freshly ground black
    pepper

TO GARNISH:
lemon slices
sprigs of fresh coriander

1 Preheat the oven to 140°C/
275°F/Gas Mark 1. Heat the
oil in a flameproof casserole with
a tight-fitting lid and add the
almonds. Cook for about 1
minute until just starting to
brown, stirring often. Add the
onion, carrot and celery and cook
gently for a further 8–10 minutes
until soft and lightly browned.

2 Increase the heat and add
the lamb. Cook for a further
5 minutes until the lamb has
changed colour. Add the ground
cinnamon and chilli flakes and
stir briefly before adding the
tomatoes and orange rind.

3 Stir and add the rice, then
the stock. Bring slowly to the
boil and cover tightly. Transfer to
the preheated oven and cook for
30–35 minutes until the rice is
tender and the stock is absorbed.

4 Remove from the oven and
leave to stand for 5 minutes
before stirring in the chives and
coriander. Season to taste with
salt and pepper. Garnish with the
lemon slices and sprigs of fresh
coriander and serve immediately.

TASTY TIP

The lamb in this aromatic
pilaf is cooked for a relatively
short time, so choose a
tender cut such as leg,
shoulder or fillet. If you buy
the meat on the bone, use the
bones to make a stock – it will
make all the difference to the
final flavour of the dish.

Moroccan Penne

INGREDIENTS   Serves 4

1 tbsp sunflower oil
1 red onion, peeled and
   chopped
2 cloves garlic, peeled and
   crushed
1 tbsp coriander seeds
¼ tsp cumin seeds
¼ tsp freshly grated nutmeg
450 g/1 lb lean lamb mince
1 aubergine, trimmed and
   diced

400 g can chopped tomatoes
300 ml/½ pint vegetable stock
125 g/4 oz ready-to-eat
   apricots, chopped
12 black olives, pitted
salt and freshly ground black
   pepper
350 g/12 oz penne
1 tbsp toasted pine nuts, to
   garnish

1 Preheat the oven to 200°C/
400°F/Gas Mark 6,
15 minutes before using. Heat
the sunflower oil in a large
flameproof casserole. Add the
chopped onion and fry for 5
minutes, or until softened.

2 Using a pestle and mortar,
pound the garlic, coriander
seeds, cumin seeds and grated
nutmeg together into a paste.
Add to the onion and cook for
3 minutes.

3 Add the lamb mince to the
casserole and fry, stirring
with a wooden spoon, for 4–5
minutes, or until the mince has
broken up and browned.

4 Add the aubergine to the
mince and fry for 5 minutes.
Stir in the chopped tomatoes and
vegetable stock and bring to the
boil. Add the apricots and olives,
then season well with salt and

pepper. Return to the boil,
lower the heat and simmer for
15 minutes.

5 Add the penne to the
casserole, stir well, then cover
and place in the preheated oven.
Cook for 10 minutes then stir and
return to the oven, uncovered,
for a further 15–20 minutes, or
until the pasta is 'al dente'.
Remove from the oven, sprinkle
with toasted pine nuts and serve
immediately.

TASTY TIP

You can sometimes buy pine
nuts ready-toasted, but they
are easy to do yourself.
Sprinkle them on a foil-lined
grill pan and place under a
medium grill for 3–4 minutes,
turning frequently until
they are golden-brown.

ROASTED LAMB
WITH ROSEMARY & GARLIC

INGREDIENTS   Serves 6

1.6 kg/3½ lb leg of lamb
8 garlic cloves, peeled
few sprigs of fresh rosemary
salt and freshly ground black
   pepper
4 slices pancetta
4 tbsp olive oil

4 tbsp red wine vinegar
900 g/2 lb potatoes
1 large onion
sprigs of fresh rosemary, to
   garnish
freshly cooked ratatouille,
   to serve

1 Preheat oven to 200°C/ 400°F/Gas Mark 6, 15 minutes before roasting. Wipe the leg of lamb with a clean damp cloth, then place the lamb in a large roasting tin. With a sharp knife, make small, deep incisions into the meat. Cut 2–3 garlic cloves into small slivers, then insert with a few small sprigs of rosemary into the lamb. Season to taste with salt and pepper and cover the lamb with the slices of pancetta.

2 Drizzle over 1 tablespoon of the olive oil and lay a few more rosemary sprigs across the lamb. Roast in the preheated oven for 30 minutes, then pour over the vinegar.

3 Peel the potatoes and cut into large dice. Peel the onion and cut into thick wedges then thickly slice the remaining garlic. Arrange around the lamb. Pour the remaining olive oil over the potatoes, then reduce the

oven temperature to 180°C/ 350°F/Gas Mark 4 and roast for a further 1 hour, or until the lamb is tender. Garnish with fresh sprigs of rosemary and serve immediately with the roast potatoes and ratatouille.

FOOD FACT

If you are unable to get a leg
of lamb weighing exactly
1.6 kg/3½ lb, calculate the
cooking time as follows:
20 minutes per 450 g/lb
plus 30 minutes for rare,
25 minutes per 450 g/lb plus
30 minutes for medium and
30 minutes per 450 g/lb plus
30 minutes for well done.

LANCASHIRE HOTPOT

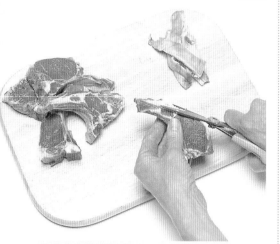

1

INGREDIENTS   Serves 4

1 kg/2¼ lb middle end neck of lamb, divided into cutlets
2 tbsp vegetable oil
2 large onions, peeled and sliced
2 tsp plain flour
150 ml/¼ pint vegetable or lamb stock
700 g/1½ lb waxy potatoes, peeled and thickly sliced

salt and freshly ground black pepper
1 bay leaf
2 sprigs of fresh thyme
1 tbsp melted butter
2 tbsp freshly chopped herbs, to garnish
freshly cooked green beans, to serve

3

1 Preheat the oven to 170°C/ 325°F/Gas Mark 3. Trim any excess fat from the lamb cutlets. Heat the oil in a frying pan and brown the cutlets in batches for 3–4 minutes. Remove with a slotted spoon and reserve. Add the onions to the frying pan and cook for 6–8 minutes until softened and just beginning to colour, then remove and reserve.

2 Stir in the flour and cook for a few seconds, then gradually pour in the stock, stirring well, and bring to the boil. Remove from the heat.

3

3 Spread the base of a large casserole with half the potato slices. Top with half the onions and season well with salt and pepper. Arrange the browned meat in a layer. Season again and add the remaining onions, bay leaf and thyme. Pour in the remaining liquid from the onions and top with remaining potatoes

so that they overlap in a single layer. Brush the potatoes with the melted butter and season again.

4 Cover the saucepan and cook in the preheated oven for 2 hours, uncovering for the last 30 minutes to allow the potatoes to brown. Garnish with chopped herbs and serve immediately with green beans.

FOOD FACT

The name of this classic dish derives from the past tradition of wrapping it in blankets after cooking to keep it warm until lunchtime. There are dozens of versions all claiming to be authentic. Some include lambs kidneys to enrich the gravy, but whatever the ingredients, it is important to season well and to cook it slowly, so that the lamb is meltingly tender.

ROAST LEG OF LAMB & BOULANGERE POTATOES

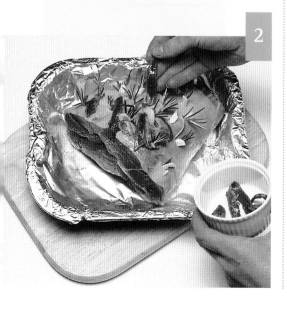

INGREDIENTS   Serves 6

1.1 kg/2½ lb potatoes, peeled
1 large onion, peeled and
  finely sliced
salt and freshly ground black
  pepper
2 tbsp olive oil
50 g/2 oz butter
200 ml/7 fl oz lamb stock

100 ml/3½ fl oz milk
2 kg/4½ lb leg of lamb
2–3 sprigs of fresh rosemary
6 large garlic cloves, peeled
  and finely sliced
6 anchovy fillets, drained
extra sprigs of fresh rosemary,
  to garnish

1 Preheat the oven to 230°C/ 450°F/Gas Mark 8. Finely slice the potatoes – a mandolin is the best tool for this. Layer the potatoes with the onion in a large roasting tin, seasoning each layer with salt and pepper. Drizzle about 1 tablespoon of the olive oil over the potatoes and add the butter in small pieces. Pour in the lamb stock and milk. Set aside.

2 Make small incisions all over the lamb with the point of a small, sharp knife. Into each incision insert a small piece of rosemary, a sliver of garlic and a piece of anchovy fillet.

3 Drizzle the leg of lamb and its flavourings with the rest of the olive oil and season well. Place the meat directly onto a shelf in the preheated oven. Position the roasting tin of potatoes directly underneath to catch the juices during cooking. Roast for 15 minutes per 500 g/ 1 lb 2 oz (about 1 hour for a joint this size), reducing the oven temperature after 20 minutes to 200°C/ 400°F/Gas Mark 6.

4 When the lamb is cooked, remove from the oven and allow to rest for 10 minutes before carving. Meanwhile, increase the oven heat and cook the potatoes for a further 10–15 minutes to crisp up. Garnish with fresh rosemary sprigs and serve immediately with the lamb.

FOOD FACT

Leg of lamb is one of the prime roasting joints and is known by its French name *gigot* in Scotland. It may weigh between 1.8–2.7 kg/ 4–6 lb, so ask for a small joint for this dish. Although home-produced lamb is at its best in the spring, there is a good supply all year round of imported New Zealand lamb.

BRAISED LAMB WITH BROAD BEANS

INGREDIENTS   Serves 4

700 g/1½ lb lamb, cut into
   large chunks
1 tbsp plain flour
1 onion
2 garlic cloves
1 tbsp olive oil
400 g can chopped tomatoes
   with basil
300 ml/½ pint lamb stock
2 tbsp freshly chopped thyme

2 tbsp freshly chopped
   oregano
salt and freshly ground black
   pepper
150 g/5 oz frozen broad beans
fresh oregano, to garnish
creamy mashed potatoes, to
   serve

1 Trim the lamb, discarding any fat or gristle, then place the flour in a polythene bag, add the lamb and toss until coated thoroughly. Peel and slice the onion and garlic and reserve. Heat the olive oil in a heavy-based saucepan and when hot, add the lamb and cook, stirring until the meat is sealed and browned all over. Using a slotted spoon transfer the lamb to a plate and reserve.

2 Add the onion and garlic to the saucepan and cook for 3 minutes, stirring frequently until softened, then return the lamb to the saucepan. Add the chopped tomatoes with their juice, the stock, the chopped thyme and oregano to the pan and season to taste with salt and pepper. Bring to the boil, then cover with a close-fitting lid, reduce the heat and simmer for 1 hour.

3 Add the broad beans to the lamb and simmer for 20–30 minutes, or until the lamb is tender. Garnish with fresh oregano and serve with creamy mashed potatoes.

FOOD FACT

If you want to use fresh broad beans in season, you will need about 450 g/1 lb of beans in their pods for this recipe. If you prefer to peel the beans, plunge them first into boiling salted water for about 30 seconds, drain and refresh under cold water. The skins will come off very easily.

GRILLED STEAKS WITH SAFFRON POTATOES & ROAST TOMATOES

INGREDIENTS · Serves 4

700 g/1½ lb new potatoes, halved
few strands of saffron
300 ml/½ pint vegetable or beef stock
1 small onion, peeled and finely chopped
75 g/3 oz butter
salt and freshly ground black pepper

2 tsp balsamic vinegar
2 tbsp olive oil
1 tsp caster sugar
8 plum tomatoes, halved
4 boneless sirloin steaks, each weighing 225 g/8 oz
2 tbsp freshly chopped parsley

1 Cook the potatoes in boiling salted water for 8 minutes and drain well. Return the potatoes to the saucepan along with the saffron, stock, onion and 25 g/1 oz of the butter. Season to taste with salt and pepper and simmer, uncovered for 10 minutes until the potatoes are tender.

2 Meanwhile, preheat the grill to medium. Mix together the vinegar, olive oil, sugar and seasoning. Arrange the tomatoes cut-side up in a foil-lined grill pan and drizzle over the dressing. Grill for 12–15 minutes, basting occasionally, until tender.

3 Melt the remaining butter in a frying pan. Add the steaks and cook for 4–8 minutes to taste and depending on thickness.

4 Arrange the potatoes and tomatoes in the centre of

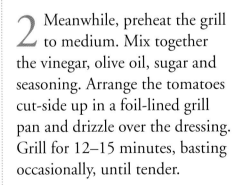

4 serving plates. Top with the steaks along with any pan juices. Sprinkle over the parsley and serve immediately.

HELPFUL HINT

You can tell how well a steak is cooked by lightly pressing with your fingertips – the less the resistance the rarer the meat. Timing depends on the thickness rather than the weight of the steak. As a rough guide a 2 cm/¾ inch thick steak will take about 2 minutes on each side for rare, 3–4 minutes on each side for medium and 6–7 minutes on each side for well-done.

FILLET STEAKS WITH TOMATO & GARLIC SAUCE

INGREDIENTS   Serves 4

700 g/1½ lb ripe tomatoes
2 garlic cloves
2 tbsp olive oil
2 tbsp freshly chopped basil
2 tbsp freshly chopped
  oregano
2 tbsp red wine
salt and freshly ground black
  pepper

75 g/3 oz pitted black olives,
  chopped
4 fillet steaks, about 175 g/6 oz
  each in weight
freshly cooked vegetables, to
  serve

1 Make a small cross on the top of each tomato and place in a large bowl. Cover with boiling water and leave for 2 minutes. Using a slotted spoon, remove the tomatoes and skin carefully. Repeat until all the tomatoes are skinned. Place on a chopping board, cut into quarters, remove the seeds and roughly chop, then reserve.

2 Peel and chop the garlic. Heat half the olive oil in a saucepan and cook the garlic for 30 seconds. Add the chopped tomatoes with the basil, oregano, red wine and season to taste with salt and pepper. Bring to the boil then reduce the heat, cover and simmer for 15 minutes, stirring occasionally, or until the sauce is reduced and thickened. Stir the olives into the sauce and keep warm while cooking the steaks.

3 Meanwhile, lightly oil a griddle pan or heavy-based frying pan with the remaining olive oil and cook the steaks for 2 minutes on each side to seal. Continue to cook the steaks for a further 2–4 minutes, depending on personal preference. Serve the steaks immediately with the garlic sauce and freshly cooked vegetables.

HELPFUL HINT

Fillet steak should be a deep mahogany colour with a good marbling of fat. If the meat is bright red or if the fat is bright white the meat has not been aged properly and will probably be quite tough.

BEEF TERIYAKI WITH GREEN & BLACK RICE

INGREDIENTS   Serves 4

3 tbsp sake (Japanese rice wine)

3 tbsp dry sherry

3 tbsp dark soy sauce

1½ tbsp soft brown sugar

4 sirloin steaks, each weighing 175 g /6 oz, trimmed

350 g/12 oz long-grain and wild rice

2.5 cm/1 inch piece fresh root ginger

225 g/8 oz mangetout

salt

6 spring onions, trimmed and cut into fine strips

1 In a small saucepan, gently heat the sake, dry sherry, dark soy sauce and sugar until the sugar has dissolved. Increase the heat and bring to the boil. Remove from the heat and leave until cold. Lightly wipe the steaks, place in a shallow dish and pour the sake mixture over. Cover loosely and leave to marinate in the refrigerator for at least 1 hour, spooning the marinade over the steaks occasionally.

2 Cook the rice with the piece of root ginger, according to the packet instructions. Drain well, then remove and discard the piece of ginger.

3 Slice the mangetout thinly lengthways into fine shreds. Plunge into a saucepan of boiling salted water, return the water to the boil and drain immediately. Stir the drained mangetout and spring onions into the hot rice.

4 Meanwhile, heat a griddle pan until almost smoking. Remove the steaks from the marinade and cook on the hot grill pan for 3–4 minutes each side, depending on the thickness.

5 Place the remaining marinade in a saucepan and bring to the boil. Simmer rapidly for 2 minutes and remove from the heat. When the steaks are cooked to personal preference, leave to rest for 2–3 minutes, then slice thinly and serve with the rice and the hot marinade.

FOOD FACT

Before 1867, meat was prohibited in Japan in the belief that it would prevent aggression. The Japanese still eat a relatively small amount of meat and tend to use quick-cook tender cuts in dishes.

MEATBALLS WITH BEAN & TOMATO SAUCE

INGREDIENTS   Serves 4

1 large onion, peeled and
  finely chopped
1 red pepper, deseeded and
  chopped
1 tbsp freshly chopped oregano
½ tsp hot paprika
425 g can red kidney beans,
  drained
300 g/11 oz fresh beef mince
salt and freshly ground black
  pepper

4 tbsp sunflower oil
1 garlic clove, peeled and
  crushed
400 g can chopped
  tomatoes
1 tbsp freshly chopped
  coriander, to garnish
freshly cooked rice, to serve

1 Make the meatballs by blending half the onion, half the red pepper, the oregano, the paprika and 350 g/12 oz of the kidney beans in a blender or food processor for a few seconds. Add the beef with seasoning and blend until well mixed. Turn the mixture onto a lightly floured board and form into small balls.

2 Heat the wok, then add 2 tablespoons of the oil and, when hot, stir-fry the meatballs gently until well browned on all sides. Remove with a slotted spoon and keep warm.

3 Wipe the wok clean, then add the remaining oil and cook the remaining onion and pepper and the garlic for 3–4 minutes, until soft. Add the tomatoes, seasoning to taste and remaining kidney beans.

4 Return the meatballs to the wok, stir them into the sauce, then cover and simmer for 10 minutes. Sprinkle with the chopped coriander and serve immediately with the freshly cooked rice.

FOOD FACT

Paprika gives this dish its distinctive flavour and colour. Made from dried peppers, it is available hot or mild and even smoked. The best paprika comes from either Hungary or Spain, where in both places it is widely used.

CHILLI CON CARNE WITH CRISPY-SKINNED POTATOES

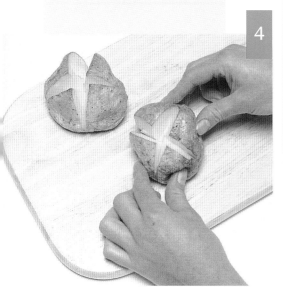

INGREDIENTS   Serves 4

2 tbsp vegetable oil, plus extra
  for brushing
1 large onion, peeled and
  finely chopped
1 garlic clove, peeled and
  finely chopped
1 red chilli, deseeded and
  finely chopped
450 g/1 lb chuck steak, finely
  chopped, or lean beef mince
1 tbsp chilli powder

400 g can chopped tomatoes
2 tbsp tomato purée
400 g can red kidney beans,
  drained and rinsed
4 large baking potatoes
coarse salt and freshly ground
  black pepper

TO SERVE:
ready-made guacamole
soured cream

1 Preheat the oven to 150°C/ 300°F/Gas Mark 2. Heat the oil in a large flameproof casserole and add the onion. Cook gently for 10 minutes until soft and lightly browned. Add the garlic and chilli and cook briefly. Increase the heat. Add the chuck steak or lean mince and cook for a further 10 minutes, stirring occasionally, until browned.

2 Add the chilli powder and stir well. Cook for about 2 minutes, then add the chopped tomatoes and tomato purée. Bring slowly to the boil. Cover and cook in the preheated oven for 1½ hours. Remove from the oven and stir in the kidney beans. Return to the oven for a further 15 minutes.

3 Meanwhile, brush a little vegetable oil all over the potatoes and rub on some coarse salt. Put the potatoes in the oven alongside the chilli.

4 Remove the chilli and potatoes from the oven. Cut a cross in each potato, then squeeze to open slightly and season to taste with salt and pepper. Serve with the chilli, guacamole and soured cream.

TASTY TIP

Make your own guacamole by peeling, stoning and mashing 1 large avocado in a bowl with 2 tablespoons each of lemon juice and crème fraîche, ¼ teaspoon Tabasco sauce, 1 crushed garlic clove and salt and pepper. Push the avocado stone into the dip to stop it from discolouring.

PASTA WITH BEEF, CAPERS & OLIVES

INGREDIENTS   Serves 4

2 tbsp olive oil

300 g/11 oz rump steak, trimmed and cut into strips

4 spring onions, trimmed and sliced

2 garlic cloves, peeled and chopped

2 courgettes, trimmed and cut into strips

1 red pepper, deseeded and cut into strips

2 tsp freshly chopped oregano

2 tbsp capers, drained and rinsed

4 tbsp pitted black olives, sliced

400 g can chopped tomatoes

salt and freshly ground black pepper

450 g/1 lb fettuccine

1 tbsp freshly chopped parsley, to garnish

1 Heat the olive oil in a large frying pan over a high heat. Add the steak and cook, stirring, for 3–4 minutes, or until browned. Remove from the pan using a slotted spoon and reserve.

2 Lower the heat, add the spring onions and garlic to the pan and cook for 1 minute. Add the courgettes and pepper and cook for 3–4 minutes.

3 Add the oregano, capers and olives to the pan with the chopped tomatoes. Season to taste with salt and pepper, then simmer for 7 minutes, stirring occasionally. Return the beef to the pan and simmer for 3–5 minutes, or until the sauce has thickened slightly.

4 Meanwhile, bring a large pan of lightly salted water to a rolling boil. Add the pasta and cook according to the packet instructions, or until 'al dente'.

5 Drain the pasta thoroughly. Return to the pan and add the beef sauce. Toss gently until the pasta is lightly coated. Tip into a warmed serving dish or on to individual plates. Sprinkle with chopped parsley and serve immediately.

HELPFUL HINT

When cooking the beef, it is important that it fries rather than steams in the pan, giving a beautifully brown and caramelised outside while keeping the middle moist and tender. Make sure that the oil in the pan is hot so that the strips of beef sizzle when added. Pat the beef dry with absorbent kitchen paper and cook it in two batches, so there is plenty of room to move it around the pan.

PASTA & PORK RAGÙ

INGREDIENTS

Serves 4

1 tbsp sunflower oil
1 leek, trimmed and thinly sliced
225 g/8 oz pork fillet, diced
1 garlic clove, peeled and crushed
2 tsp paprika
¼ tsp cayenne pepper
150 ml/¼ pint white wine
600 ml/1 pint vegetable stock

400g can borlotti beans, drained and rinsed
2 carrots, peeled and diced
salt and freshly ground black pepper
225 g/8 oz fresh egg tagliatelle
1 tbsp freshly chopped parsley, to garnish
crème fraîche, to serve

1 Heat the sunflower oil in a large frying pan. Add the sliced leek and cook, stirring frequently, for 5 minutes, or until softened. Add the pork and cook, stirring, for 4 minutes, or until sealed.

2 Add the crushed garlic and the paprika and cayenne peppers to the pan and stir until all the pork is lightly coated in the garlic and pepper mixture.

3 Pour in the wine and 450 ml/¾ pint of the vegetable stock. Add the borlotti beans and carrots and season to taste with salt and pepper. Bring the sauce to the boil, then lower the heat and simmer for 5 minutes.

4 Meanwhile, place the egg tagliatelle in a large saucepan of lightly salted, boiling water, cover and simmer for 5 minutes, or until the pasta is cooked 'al dente'.

5 Drain the pasta, then add to the pork ragù; toss well. Adjust the seasoning, then tip into a warmed serving dish. Sprinkle with chopped parsley and serve with a little crème fraîche.

HELPFUL HINT

Pork fillet, also known as tenderloin, is a very lean and tender cut of pork. It needs little cooking time, so is perfect for this quick and simple dish. Rump or sirloin steak or boneless skinned chicken breast, cut into thin strips, could be used instead, if preferred.

CARIBBEAN PORK

INGREDIENTS Serves 4

450 g/1 lb pork fillet
2.5 cm/1 inch piece fresh root
  ginger, peeled and grated
½ tsp crushed dried chillies
2 garlic cloves, peeled and
  crushed
2 tbsp freshly chopped parsley
150 ml/¼ pint orange juice
2 tbsp dark soy sauce
2 tbsp groundnut oil

1 large onion, peeled and
  sliced into wedges
1 large courgette (about
  225 g/8 oz), trimmed and
  cut into strips
1 orange pepper, deseeded
  and cut into strips
1 ripe but firm mango, peeled
  and pitted
freshly cooked rice to serve

1 Cut the pork fillet into thin strips and place in a shallow dish. Sprinkle with the ginger, chillies, garlic and 1 tablespoon of the parsley. Blend together the orange juice, soy sauce and 1 tablespoon of the oil, then pour over the pork. Cover and chill in the refrigerator for 30 minutes, stirring occasionally. Remove the pork strips with a slotted spoon and reserve the marinade.

2 Heat the wok, pour in the remaining oil and stir-fry the pork for 3–4 minutes. Add the onion rings and the courgette and pepper strips and cook for 2 minutes. Add the reserved marinade to the wok and stir-fry for a further 2 minutes.

3 Remove the stone from the mango, cut the flesh into strips, then stir it into the pork mixture. Continue to stir-fry

until everything is piping hot. Garnish with the remaining parsley and serve immediately with plenty of freshly cooked rice.

HELPFUL HINT

Pork fillet, or tenderloin, as it is sometimes known, is a very tender cut and is always boneless. It may have some sinew attached and this should be removed with a sharp knife.

HONEY PORK WITH RICE NOODLES & CASHEWS

INGREDIENTS   Serves 4

125 g/4 oz rice noodles	3 tbsp clear honey
450 g/1 lb pork fillet	50 g/2 oz unsalted cashew
2 tbsp groundnut oil	nuts
1 tbsp softened butter	1 red chilli, deseeded and
1 onion, peeled and finely	finely chopped
sliced into rings	4 spring onions, trimmed
2 garlic cloves, peeled and	and finely chopped
crushed	freshly stir-fried vegetables,
125 g/4 oz baby button	to serve
mushrooms, halved	
3 tbsp light soy sauce	

1 Soak the rice noodles in boiling water for 4 minutes or according to packet instructions, then drain and reserve.

2 Trim and slice the pork fillet into thin strips. Heat the wok, pour in the oil and butter, and stir-fry the pork for 4–5 minutes, until cooked. Remove with a slotted spoon and keep warm.

3 Add the onion to the wok and stir-fry gently for 2 minutes. Stir in the garlic and mushrooms and cook for a further 2 minutes, or until juices start to run from the mushrooms.

4 Blend the soy sauce with the honey then return the pork to the wok with this mixture. Add the cashew nuts and cook for 1–2 minutes, then add the rice noodles a little at a time. Stir-

fry until everything is piping hot. Sprinkle with chopped chilli and spring onions. Serve immediately with freshly stir-fried vegetables.

TASTY TIP

Heat a wok until really hot, then add 1 tablespoon of oil. Carefully swirl around the wok, then add 1 chopped garlic clove and a little grated ginger. Add a finely sliced red, green and yellow pepper, some mangetout and spring onion. Stir-fry for 3–4 minutes, then serve with the pork.

PORK MEATBALLS WITH VEGETABLES

INGREDIENTS   Serves 4

450 g/1 lb pork mince
2 tbsp freshly chopped
  coriander
2 garlic cloves, peeled and
  chopped
1 tbsp light soy sauce
salt and freshly ground black
  pepper
2 tbsp groundnut oil
2 cm/1 inch piece fresh root
  ginger, peeled and cut into
  matchsticks
1 red pepper, deseeded and
  cut into chunks

1 green pepper, deseeded and
  cut into chunks
2 courgettes, trimmed and cut
  into sticks
125 g/4 oz baby sweetcorn,
  halved lengthways
3 tbsp light soy sauce
1 tsp sesame oil
fresh coriander leaves, to
  garnish
freshly cooked noodles, to
  serve

1 Mix together the pork mince, the chopped coriander, half the garlic and the soy sauce, then season to taste with salt and pepper. Divide into 20 portions and roll into balls. Place on a baking sheet, cover with clingfilm and chill in the refrigerator for at least 30 minutes.

2 Heat a wok or large frying pan, add the groundnut oil and when hot, add the meatballs and cook for 8–10 minutes, or until the pork balls are browned all over, turning occasionally. Using a slotted spoon, transfer the balls to a plate and keep warm.

3 Add the ginger and remaining garlic to the wok and stir-fry for 30 seconds. Add the red and green peppers and stir-fry for 5 minutes. Add the courgettes and sweetcorn and stir-fry for 3 minutes.

4 Return the pork balls to the wok, add the soy sauce and sesame oil and stir-fry for 1 minute, until heated through. Garnish with coriander leaves and serve immediately on a bed of noodles.

HELPFUL HINT

Chilling the meatballs firms and helps prevent them breaking up during cooking. If you find it easier, cook the pork balls in 2 batches.

JAMAICAN JERK PORK WITH RICE & PEAS

INGREDIENTS   Serves 4

175 g/6 oz dried red kidney
  beans, soaked overnight
2 onions, peeled and chopped
2 garlic cloves, peeled and
  crushed
4 tbsp lime juice
2 tbsp each dark molasses,
  soy sauce and chopped fresh
  root ginger
2 jalapeño chillies, deseeded
  and chopped
½ tsp ground cinnamon
¼ tsp each ground allspice,
  ground nutmeg
4 pork loin chops, on the bone

FOR THE RICE:
1 tbsp vegetable oil
1 onion, peeled and finely
  chopped
1 celery stalk, trimmed and
  finely sliced
3 garlic cloves, peeled and
  crushed
2 bay leaves
225 g/8 oz long-grain white
  rice
475 ml/18 fl oz chicken or ham
  stock
sprigs of fresh flat-leaf parsley,
  to garnish

1 To make the jerk pork marinade, purée the onions, garlic, lime juice, molasses, soy sauce, ginger, chillies, cinnamon, allspice and nutmeg together in a food processor until smooth. Put the pork chops into a plastic or non-reactive dish and pour over the marinade, turning the chops to coat. Marinate in the refrigerator for at least 1 hour or overnight.

2 Drain the beans and place in a large saucepan with about 2 litres/3½ pints cold water. Bring to the boil and boil rapidly for 10 minutes. Reduce the heat, cover and simmer gently, for 1 hour until tender, adding more water, if necessary. When cooked, drain well and mash roughly.

3 Heat the oil for the rice in a saucepan with a tight-fitting lid and add the onion, celery and garlic. Cook gently for 5 minutes until softened. Add the bay leaves, rice and stock and stir. Bring to the boil, cover and cook very gently for 10 minutes. Add the beans and stir well again. Cook for a further 5 minutes, then remove from the heat.

4 Heat a griddle pan until almost smoking. Remove the pork chops from the marinade, scraping off any surplus and add to the hot pan. Cook for 5–8 minutes on each side, or until cooked. Garnish with the parsley and serve immediately with the rice.

PORK GOULASH & RICE

INGREDIENTS
Serves 4

700 g/1½ lb boneless pork rib chops
1 tbsp olive oil
2 onions, peeled and roughly chopped
1 red pepper, deseeded and sliced thinly
1 garlic clove, peeled and crushed
1 tbsp plain flour

1 rounded tbsp paprika
400 g can chopped tomatoes
salt and freshly ground black pepper
250 g/9 oz long-grain white rice
450 ml/¾ pint chicken stock
sprigs of fresh flat-leaf parsley, to garnish
150 ml/¼ pint soured cream, to serve

1 Preheat the oven to 140°C/ 275°F/Gas Mark 1. Cut the pork into large cubes, about 4 cm/1½ inches square. Heat the oil in a large flameproof casserole and brown the pork in batches over a high heat, transferring the cubes to a plate as they brown.

2 Over a medium heat, add the onions and pepper and cook for about 5 minutes, stirring regularly, until they begin to brown. Add the garlic and return the meat to the casserole along with any juices on the plate. Sprinkle in the flour and paprika and stir well to soak up the oil and juices.

3 Add the tomatoes and season to taste with salt and pepper. Bring slowly to the boil, cover with a tight-fitting lid and cook in the preheated oven for 1½ hours.

4 Meanwhile, rinse the rice in several changes of water until

the water remains relatively clear. Drain well and put into a saucepan with the chicken stock or water and a little salt. Cover tightly and bring to the boil. Turn the heat down as low as possible and cook for 10 minutes without removing the lid. After 10 minutes, remove from the heat and leave for a further 10 minutes, without removing the lid. Fluff with a fork.

5 When the meat is tender, stir in the soured cream lightly to create a marbled effect, or serve separately. Garnish with parsley and serve immediately with the rice.

FOOD FACT

Paprika is the ground red powder from the dried pepper *Capsicum annum* and is a vital ingredient of goulash, giving it a distinctive colour and taste.

SPANISH-STYLE PORK STEW WITH SAFFRON RICE

INGREDIENTS   Serves 4

2 tbsp olive oil

900 g/2 lb boneless pork shoulder, diced

1 large onion, peeled and sliced

2 garlic cloves, peeled and finely chopped

1 tbsp plain flour

450 g/1 lb plum tomatoes, peeled and chopped

175 ml/6 fl oz red wine

1 tbsp freshly chopped basil

1 green pepper, deseeded and sliced

50 g/2 oz pimiento-stuffed olives, cut in half crossways

salt and freshly ground black pepper

fresh basil leaves, to garnish

FOR THE SAFFRON RICE:

1 tbsp olive oil

25 g/1 oz butter

1 small onion, peeled and finely chopped

few strands of saffron, crushed

250 g/9 oz long-grain white rice

600 ml/1 pint chicken stock

1 Preheat the oven to 150°C/ 300°F/Gas Mark 2. Heat the oil in a large flameproof casserole and add the pork in batches. Fry over a high heat until browned. Transfer to a plate until all the pork is browned.

2 Lower the heat and add the onion to the casserole. Cook for a further 5 minutes until soft and starting to brown. Add the garlic and stir briefly before returning the pork to the casserole. Add the flour and stir.

3 Add the tomatoes. Gradually stir in the red wine and add the basil. Bring to simmering point and cover. Transfer the casserole to the lower part of the preheated oven and cook for 1½ hours. Stir in the green pepper and olives and cook for 30 minutes. Season to taste with salt and pepper.

4 Meanwhile, to make the saffron rice, heat the oil with the butter in a saucepan. Add the onion and cook for 5 minutes over a medium heat until softened. Add the saffron and rice and stir well. Add the stock, bring to the boil, cover and reduce the heat as low as possible. Cook for 15 minutes, covered, until the rice is tender and the stock is absorbed. Adjust the seasoning and serve with the stew, garnished with fresh basil.

LEEK & HAM RISOTTO

INGREDIENTS   Serves 4

1 tbsp olive oil
25 g/1 oz butter
1 medium onion, peeled and
  finely chopped
4 leeks, trimmed and thinly
  sliced
1½ tbsp freshly chopped
  thyme
350 g/12 oz Arborio rice

1.4 litres/2¼ pints vegetable or
  chicken stock, heated
225 g/8 oz cooked ham
175 g/6 oz peas, thawed if
  frozen
50 g/2 oz Parmesan cheese,
  grated
salt and freshly ground black
  pepper

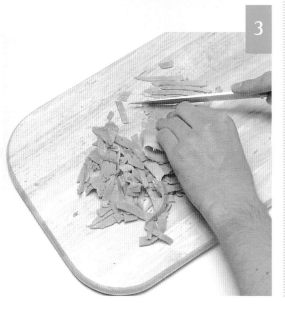

1 Heat the oil and half the butter together in a large saucepan. Add the onion and leeks and cook over a medium heat for 6–8 minutes, stirring occasionally, until soft and beginning to colour. Stir in the thyme and cook briefly.

2 Add the rice and stir well. Continue stirring over a medium heat for about 1 minute until the rice is glossy. Add a ladleful or two of the stock and stir well until the stock is absorbed. Continue adding stock, a ladleful at a time, and stirring well between additions, until about two-thirds of the stock has been added.

3 Meanwhile, either chop or finely shred the ham, then add to the saucepan of rice together with the peas. Continue adding ladlefuls of stock, as described in step 2, until the rice is tender and the ham is heated through thoroughly.

4 Add the remaining butter, sprinkle over the Parmesan cheese and season to taste with salt and pepper. When the butter has melted and the cheese has softened, stir well to incorporate. Taste and adjust the seasoning, then serve immediately.

HELPFUL HINT

Risotto should take about 15 minutes to cook, so taste it after this time – the rice should be creamy with just a slight bite to it. If it is not quite ready, continue adding the stock, a little at a time, and cook for a few more minutes. Stop as soon as it tastes ready as you do not have to add all of the liquid.

CHICKEN CACCIATORE

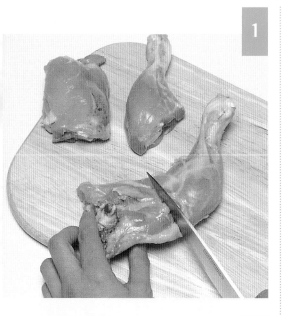

INGREDIENTS   Serves 4

4 chicken leg portions
1 tbsp olive oil
1 red onion, peeled and cut
   into very thin wedges
1 garlic clove, peeled
   and crushed
sprig of fresh thyme
sprig of fresh rosemary
150 ml/¼ pint dry white wine
200 ml/7 fl oz chicken stock
400 g can chopped tomatoes

40 g/1½ oz black
   olives, pitted
15 g/½ oz capers, drained
salt and freshly ground
   black pepper
freshly cooked fettuccine,
   linguine or pasta shells

1 Skin the chicken portions and cut each one into 2 pieces to make 4 thighs and 4 drumsticks.

2 Heat 2 teaspoons of the oil in a flameproof casserole and cook the chicken for 2–3 minutes on each side until lightly browned. Remove the chicken from the pan and reserve.

3 Add the remaining 1 teaspoon of oil to the juices in the pan.

4 Add the red onion and gently cook for 5 minutes, stirring occasionally.

5 Add the garlic and cook for a further 5 minutes until soft and beginning to brown. Return the chicken to the pan.

6 Add the herbs, then pour in the wine and let it bubble for 1–2 minutes.

7 Add the stock and tomatoes, cover and gently simmer for 15 minutes.

8 Stir in the olives and capers. Cook uncovered for a further 5 minutes or until the chicken is cooked and the sauce thickened. Remove the herbs and season to taste with salt and pepper.

9 Place the chicken on a bed of pasta, allowing one thigh and one drumstick per person. Spoon over the sauce and serve.

HELPFUL HINT

When watching your saturated fat intake, it is essential to remove the skin from the chicken before eating. Any fat is deposited directly underneath the skin.

LEMON CHICKEN WITH POTATOES, ROSEMARY & OLIVES

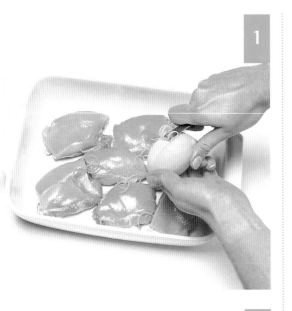

INGREDIENTS   Serves 6

12 skinless boneless chicken thighs

1 large lemon

125 ml/4 fl oz extra-virgin olive oil

6 garlic cloves, peeled and sliced

2 onions, peeled and thinly sliced

bunch of fresh rosemary

1.1 kg/2 ½ lb potatoes, peeled and cut into 4 cm/1½ inch pieces

salt and freshly ground black pepper

18–24 black olives, pitted

TO SERVE:

steamed carrots

courgettes

1 Preheat oven to 200°C/ 400°F/Gas Mark 6, 15 minutes before cooking. Trim the chicken thighs and place in a shallow baking dish large enough to hold them in a single layer. Remove the rind from the lemon with a zester or if using a peeler cut into thin julienne strips. Reserve half and add the remainder to the chicken. Squeeze the lemon juice over the chicken, toss to coat well and leave to stand for 10 minutes.

2 Transfer the chicken to a roasting tin. Add the remaining lemon zest or julienne strips, olive oil, garlic, onions and half of the rosemary sprigs. Toss gently and leave for about 20 minutes.

3 Cover the potatoes with lightly salted water and bring to the boil. Cook for 2 minutes,

then drain well and add to the chicken. Season to taste with salt and pepper.

4 Roast the chicken in the preheated oven for 50 minutes, turning frequently and basting, or until the chicken is cooked. Just before the end of cooking time, discard the rosemary, and add fresh sprigs of rosemary. Add the olives and stir. Serve immediately with steamed carrots and courgettes.

TASTY TIP

It is worth seeking out unwaxed lemons for this recipe, or for any recipe in which the lemon zest is to be eaten. If unwaxed fruit are unavailable, pour hot water over them and scrub well before removing the zest.

STEAMED, CRISPY, CITRUS CHICKEN

INGREDIENTS   Serves 6

200 ml/7 fl oz light soy sauce

1 tbsp brown sugar

4 star anise

2 slices fresh root ginger, peeled

5 spring onions, trimmed and sliced

1 small orange, cut into wedges

1 lime, cut into wedges

1.1 kg/2 ½ lb chicken

2 garlic cloves, peeled and finely chopped

2 tbsp Chinese rice wine

2 tbsp dark soy sauce

300 ml/½ pint groundnut oil

orange slices, to garnish

freshly cooked steamed rice, to serve

1 Pour the light soy sauce and 200 ml/7 fl oz water into the wok and add the sugar and star anise. Bring to the boil over a gentle heat. Pour into a small bowl and leave to cool slightly. Wipe the wok clean with absorbent kitchen paper.

2 Put the ginger, 2 spring onions, orange and lime inside the cavity of the chicken. Place a rack in the wok and pour in boiling water to a depth of 5 cm/2 inches. Put a piece of tinfoil onto the rack and place the chicken in the centre, then pour over the soy sauce mixture.

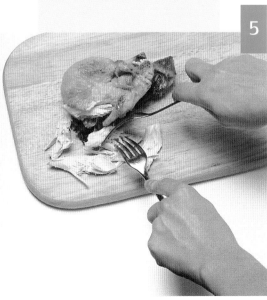

3 Cover the wok and steam gently for 1–1 hour 10 minutes, or until the chicken is cooked through, pouring off excess fat from time to time. Add more water if necessary. Leave the chicken to cool and dry for up to 3 hours, then cut the chicken into quarters.

4 Mix together the garlic, Chinese rice wine, dark soy sauce and remaining spring onions, then reserve. Dry the wok and heat again, then add the oil. When hot, shallow fry the chicken quarters for 4 minutes, or until golden and crisp. Do this 1 portion at a time, remove and drain on absorbent kitchen paper.

5 When cool enough to handle shred into bite-sized pieces and drizzle over the sauce. Garnish with slices of orange and serve with freshly steamed rice.

TASTY TIP

If you prefer, serve the shredded chicken with ready-made Chinese pancakes which have been spread with a little hoisin sauce. Top with shredded spring onions and cucumber and roll up.

CHICKEN & SUMMER VEGETABLE RISOTTO

INGREDIENTS   Serves 4

1 litre/1¾ pint chicken or vegetable stock

225 g/8 oz baby asparagus spears

125 g/4 oz French beans

15 g/½ oz butter

1 small onion, peeled and finely chopped

150 ml/¼ pint dry white wine

275 g/10 oz arborio rice

pinch of saffron strands

75 g/3 oz frozen peas, thawed

225 g/8 oz cooked chicken, skinned and diced

juice of ½ lemon

salt and freshly ground black pepper

25 g/1 oz Parmesan, shaved

1 Bring the stock to the boil in a large saucepan. Trim the asparagus and cut into 4 cm/ 1½ inch lengths.

2 Blanch the asparagus in the stock for 1–2 minutes or until tender, then remove with a slotted spoon and reserve.

3 Halve the green beans and cook in the boiling stock for 4 minutes. Remove and reserve. Turn down the heat and keep the stock barely simmering.

4 Melt the butter in a heavy-based saucepan. Add the onion and cook gently for about 5 minutes.

5 Pour the wine into the pan and boil rapidly until the liquid has almost reduced. Add the rice and cook, stirring for 1 minute until the grains are coated and look translucent.

6 Add the saffron and a ladle of the stock. Simmer, stirring all the time, until the stock has absorbed. Continue adding the stock, a ladle at a time, until it has all been absorbed.

7 After 15 minutes the risotto should be creamy with a slight bite to it. If not add a little more stock and cook for a few more minutes, or until it is of the correct texture and consistency.

8 Add the peas, reserved vegetables, chicken and lemon juice. Season to taste with salt and pepper and cook for 3-4 minutes or until the chicken is thoroughly heated and piping hot.

9 Spoon the risotto on to warmed serving plates. Scatter each portion with a few shavings of Parmesan cheese and serve immediately.

POACHED CHICKEN WITH SALSA VERDE HERB SAUCE

INGREDIENTS   Serves 6

6 boneless chicken breasts,
  each about 175 g /6 oz
600 ml/1 pint chicken stock,
  preferably homemade

FOR THE SALSA VERDE:
2 garlic cloves, peeled and
  chopped
4 tbsp freshly chopped parsley
3 tbsp freshly chopped mint
2 tsp capers
2 tbsp chopped gherkins
  (optional)

2–3 anchovy fillets in olive oil,
  drained and finely chopped
  (optional)
1 handful wild rocket leaves,
  chopped (optional)
2 tbsp lemon juice or red wine
  vinegar
125 ml/4 fl oz extra-virgin
  olive oil
salt and freshly ground black
  pepper
sprigs of mint, to garnish
freshly cooked vegetables, to
  serve

1 Place the chicken breasts with the stock in a large frying pan and bring to the boil. Reduce the heat and simmer for 10–15 minutes, or until cooked. Leave to cool in the stock.

2 To make the salsa verde, switch the motor on a food processor, then drop in the garlic cloves and chop finely. Add the parsley and mint and, using the pulse button, pulse 2–3 times. Add the capers and, if using, add the gherkins, anchovies and rocket. Pulse 2–3 times until the sauce is evenly textured.

3 With the machine still running, pour in the lemon juice or red wine vinegar, then add the olive oil in a slow, steady stream until the sauce is smooth. Season to taste with salt and pepper, then transfer to a large serving bowl and reserve.

4 Carve each chicken breast into thick slices and arrange on serving plates, fanning out the slices slightly. Spoon over a little of the salsa verde on to each chicken breast, garnish with sprigs of mint and serve immediately with freshly cooked vegetables.

FOOD FACT

The salsa verde can be made ahead and stored in an airtight container for 1 day. Be sure to bring to room temperature and stir well before serving.

CHICKEN IN BLACK BEAN SAUCE

INGREDIENTS   Serves 4

450 g/1 lb skinless, boneless chicken breast fillets, cut into strips
1 tbsp light soy sauce
2 tbsp Chinese rice wine or dry sherry
salt
1 tsp caster sugar
1 tsp sesame oil
2 tsp cornflour
2 tbsp sunflower oil
2 green peppers, deseeded and diced
1 tbsp freshly grated root ginger

2 garlic cloves, peeled and roughly chopped
2 shallots, peeled and finely chopped
4 spring onions, trimmed and finely sliced
3 tbsp salted black beans, chopped
150 ml/¼ pint chicken stock
shredded spring onions, to garnish
freshly cooked egg noodles, to serve

1 Place the chicken strips in a large bowl. Mix together the soy sauce, Chinese rice wine or sherry, a little salt, caster sugar, sesame oil and cornflour and pour over the chicken.

2 Heat the wok over a high heat, add the oil and when very hot, add the chicken strips and stir-fry for 2 minutes. Add the green peppers and stir-fry for a further 2 minutes. Then add the ginger, garlic, shallots, spring onions and black beans and continue to stir-fry for another 2 minutes.

3 Add 4 tablespoons of the stock, stir-fry for 1 minute, then pour in the remaining stock and bring to the boil. Reduce the heat and simmer the sauce for 3–4 minutes, or until the

chicken is cooked and the sauce has thickened slightly. Garnish with the shredded spring onions and serve immediately with noodles.

FOOD FACT

Black beans, also known as salted black beans, are soya beans that have been preserved by being fermented with salt and spices. They have a distinctive salty taste, a rich savoury aroma and are often used as a seasoning in conjunction with garlic or ginger. Buy the beans either in cans, in which case they will need rinsing and draining, or dry in bags. Dried black beans will keep indefinitely in an airtight container.

CHICKEN PARCELS WITH COURGETTES & PASTA

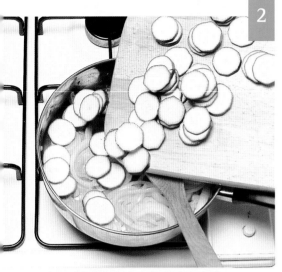

2

3

4

INGREDIENTS   Serves 4

2 tbsp olive oil

125 g/4 oz farfalle pasta

1 onion, peeled and thinly
  sliced

1 garlic clove, peeled and
  finely chopped

2 medium courgettes,
  trimmed and thinly sliced

salt and freshly ground black
  pepper

2 tbsp freshly chopped
  oregano

4 plum tomatoes, deseeded
  and coarsely chopped

4 x 175 g/6 oz boneless,
  skinless chicken breasts

150 ml/¼ pint Italian white wine

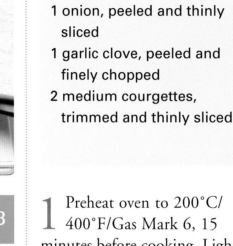

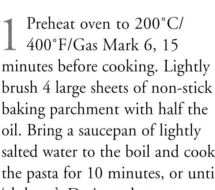

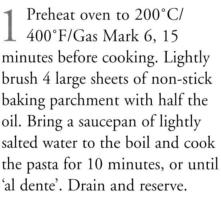

1 Preheat oven to 200°C/
400°F/Gas Mark 6, 15
minutes before cooking. Lightly
brush 4 large sheets of non-stick
baking parchment with half the
oil. Bring a saucepan of lightly
salted water to the boil and cook
the pasta for 10 minutes, or until
'al dente'. Drain and reserve.

2 Heat the remaining oil in
a frying pan and cook the
onion for 2–3 minutes. Add the
garlic and cook for 1 minute.
Add the courgettes and cook for
1 minute, then remove from the
heat, season to taste with salt and
pepper and add half the oregano.

3 Divide the cooked pasta
equally between the 4 sheets
of baking parchment, positioning
the pasta in the centre. Top the
pasta with equal amounts of the
vegetable mixture, and sprinkle a
quarter of the chopped tomatoes
over each.

4 Score the surface of each
chicken breast about 1 cm/
½ inch deep. Place a chicken
breast on top of the pasta
and sprinkle each with the
remaining oregano and the
white wine. Fold the edges
of the paper along the top,
then along each side, creating
a sealed envelope.

5 Bake in the preheated oven
for 30–35 minutes, or until
cooked. Serve immediately.

FOOD FACT

This is a great recipe for
entertaining. The parcels
can be prepared ahead and
baked when needed. For
a dramatic presentation,
serve in the paper.

Herb-baked Chicken with Tagliatelle

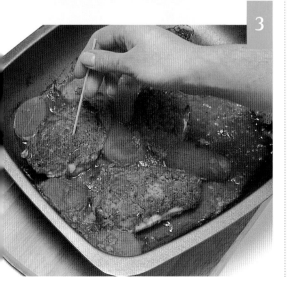

INGREDIENTS   Serves 4

75 g/3 oz fresh white
   breadcrumbs
3 tbsp olive oil
1 tsp dried oregano
2 tbsp sun-dried tomato
   paste
salt and freshly ground black
   pepper

4 boneless and skinless
   chicken breasts, each about
   150 g/5 oz
2 x 400 g cans plum tomatoes
4 tbsp freshly chopped basil
2 tbsp dry white wine
350 g/12 oz tagliatelle
fresh basil sprigs, to garnish

1 Preheat the oven to 200°C/ 400°F/Gas Mark 6, 15 minute before cooking. Mix together the breadcrumbs, 1 tablespoon of the olive oil, the oregano and tomato paste. Season to taste with salt and pepper. Place the chicken breasts well apart in a roasting tin and coat with the breadcrumb mixture.

2 Mix the plum tomatoes with the chopped basil and white wine. Season to taste, then spoon evenly round the chicken.

3 Drizzle the remaining olive oil over the chicken breasts and cook in the preheated oven for 20–30 minutes, or until the chicken is golden and the juices run clear when a skewer is inserted into the flesh.

4 Meanwhile, bring a large pan of lightly salted water to a rolling boil. Add the pasta and cook according to the packet instructions, or until 'al dente'.

5 Drain the pasta thoroughly and transfer to warmed serving plates. Arrange the chicken breasts on top of the pasta and spoon over the sauce. Garnish with sprigs of basil and serve immediately.

FOOD FACT

Sun-dried tomatoes are ripened on the vine, then split open and dried in the sun to give a deep, concentrated caramelised flavour. Sun-dried tomato paste usually comes in glass jars, but can also be found in tubes. Once opened, store in the refrigerator and, if in a jar, cover the surface with a teaspoonful of olive oil to keep fresh.

PERSIAN CHICKEN PILAF

INGREDIENTS   Serves 4–6

2–3 tbsp vegetable oil
700 g/1½ lb boneless skinless
  chicken pieces (breast and
  thighs), cut into 2.5 cm/
  1 inch pieces
2 medium onions, peeled and
  coarsely chopped
1 tsp ground cumin
200 g/7 oz long-grain white
  rice
1 tbsp tomato purée
1 tsp saffron strands

salt and freshly ground black
  pepper
100 ml/3½ fl oz pomegranate
  juice
900 ml/1½ pints chicken stock
125 g/4 oz ready-to-eat dried
  apricots or prunes, halved
2 tbsp raisins
2 tbsp freshly chopped mint or
  parsley
pomegranate seeds, to
  garnish (optional)

1 Heat the oil in a large heavy-based saucepan over a medium-high heat. Cook the chicken pieces, in batches, until lightly browned. Return all the browned chicken to the saucepan.

2 Add the onions to the saucepan, reduce the heat to medium and cook for 3–5 minutes, stirring frequently, until the onions begin to soften. Add the cumin and rice and stir to coat the rice. Cook for about 2 minutes until the rice is golden and translucent. Stir in the tomato purée and the saffron strands, then season to taste with salt and pepper.

3 Add the pomegranate juice and stock and bring to the boil, stirring once or twice. Add the apricots or prunes and raisins and stir gently. Reduce the heat to low and cook for 30 minutes until the chicken and rice are tender and the liquid is absorbed.

4 Turn into a shallow serving dish and sprinkle with the chopped mint or parsley. Serve immediately, garnished with pomegranate seeds, if using.

HELPFUL HINT

Pomegranate juice is available from Middle Eastern groceries and some specialty shops. You can extract juice from fresh pomegranates by separating the seeds from the bitter pith and membranes, then crushing the seeds in a sieve placed over a bowl. Substitute unsweetened grape or apple juice if you can not get pomegranates.

STIR-FRIED CHICKEN WITH SPINACH, TOMATOES & PINE NUTS

INGREDIENTS   Serves 4

50 g/2 oz pine nuts
2 tbsp sunflower oil
1 red onion, peeled and finely chopped
450 g/1 lb skinless, boneless chicken breast fillets, cut into strips
450 g/1 lb cherry tomatoes, halved
225 g/8 oz baby spinach, washed

salt and freshly ground black pepper
¼ tsp freshly grated nutmeg
2 tbsp balsamic vinegar
50 g/2 oz raisins
freshly cooked ribbon noodles tossed in butter, to serve

1 Heat the wok and add the pine nuts. Dry-fry for about 2 minutes, shaking often to ensure that they toast but do not burn. Remove and reserve. Wipe any dust from the wok.

2 Heat the wok again, add the oil and when hot, add the red onion and stir-fry for 2 minutes. Add the chicken and stir-fry for 2–3 minutes, or until golden brown. Reduce the heat, toss in the cherry tomatoes and stir-fry gently until the tomatoes start to disintegrate.

3 Add the baby spinach and stir-fry for 2–3 minutes, or until they start to wilt. Season to taste with salt and pepper, then sprinkle in the grated nutmeg and drizzle in the balsamic vinegar. Finally, stir in the raisins and reserved toasted pine nuts. Serve immediately on a bed of buttered ribbon noodles.

HELPFUL HINT

Baby spinach is available ready to use in bags, sold in most supermarkets. It has a more subtle, creamier flavour than larger-leaved spinach and cooks very quickly.

CHICKEN & WHITE WINE RISOTTO

INGREDIENTS   Serves 4–6

2 tbsp oil
125 g/4 oz unsalted butter
2 shallots, peeled and finely
   chopped
300 g/11 oz Arborio rice
600 ml/1 pint dry white wine
750 ml/1¼ pints chicken stock,
   heated
350 g/12 oz skinless chicken
   breast fillets, thinly sliced

50 g/2 oz Parmesan cheese,
   grated
2 tbsp freshly chopped dill or
   parsley
salt and freshly ground black
   pepper

1 Heat the oil and half the butter in a large heavy-based saucepan over a medium-high heat. Add the shallots and cook for 2 minutes, or until softened, stirring frequently. Add the rice and cook for 2–3 minutes, stirring frequently, until the rice is translucent and well coated.

2 Pour in half the wine; it will bubble and steam rapidly. Cook, stirring constantly, until the liquid is absorbed. Add a ladleful of the hot stock and cook until the liquid is absorbed. Carefully stir in the chicken.

3 Continue adding the stock, about half a ladleful at a time, allowing each addition to be absorbed before adding the next; never allow the rice to cook dry. This process should take about 20 minutes. The risotto should have a creamy consistency and the rice should be tender, but firm to the bite.

4 Stir in the remaining wine and cook for 2–3 minutes. Remove from the heat and stir in the remaining butter with the Parmesan cheese and half the chopped herbs. Season to taste with salt and pepper. Spoon into warmed shallow bowls and sprinkle each with the remaining chopped herbs. Serve immediately.

HELPFUL HINT

Keep the stock to be added to the risotto at a low simmer in a separate saucepan, so that it is piping hot when added to the rice. This will ensure that the dish is kept at a constant heat during cooking, which is important to achieve a perfect creamy texture.

CHICKEN & BABY VEGETABLE STIR FRY

INGREDIENTS   Serves 4

2 tbsp groundnut oil

1 small red chilli, deseeded and finely chopped

150 g/5 oz chicken breast or thigh meat, skinned and cut into cubes

2 baby leeks, trimmed and sliced

12 asparagus spears, halved

125 g/4 oz mangetout peas, trimmed

125 g/4 oz baby carrots, trimmed and halved lengthways

125 g/4 oz fine green beans, trimmed and diagonally sliced

125 g/4 oz baby sweetcorn, diagonally halved

50 ml/2 fl oz chicken stock

2 tsp light soy sauce

1 tbsp dry sherry

1 tsp sesame oil

toasted sesame seeds, to garnish

1 Heat the wok until very hot and add the oil. Add the chopped chilli and chicken and stir-fry for 4–5 minutes, or until the chicken is cooked and golden.

2 Increase the heat, add the leeks to the chicken and stir-fry for 2 minutes. Add the asparagus spears, mangetout peas, baby carrots, green beans, and baby sweetcorn. Stir-fry for 3–4 minutes, or until the vegetables soften slightly but still retain a slight crispness.

3 In a small bowl, mix together the chicken stock, soy sauce, dry sherry and sesame oil. Pour into the wok, stir and cook until heated through. Sprinkle with the toasted sesame seeds and serve immediately.

HELPFUL HINT

Look for packs of mixed baby vegetables in the supermarket. They are often available ready-trimmed and will save a lot of time.

CHICKEN & NEW POTATOES ON ROSEMARY SKEWERS

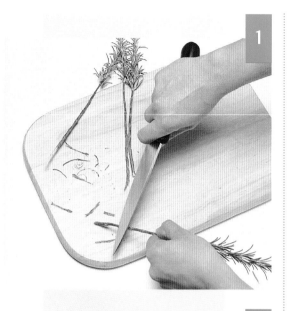

INGREDIENTS   Serves 4

8 thick fresh rosemary stems, at least 23 cm/9 inches long

3–4 tbsp extra-virgin olive oil

2 garlic cloves, peeled and crushed

1 tsp freshly chopped thyme

grated rind and juice of 1 lemon

salt and freshly ground black pepper

4 skinless chicken breast fillets

16 small new potatoes, peeled or scrubbed

8 very small onions or shallots, peeled

1 large yellow or red pepper, deseeded

lemon wedges, to garnish

parsley-flavoured cooked rice, to serve

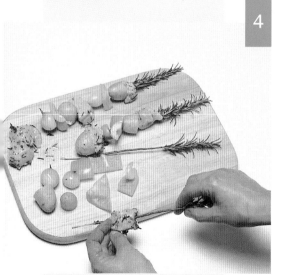

1 Preheat the grill and line the grill rack with tinfoil just before cooking. If using a barbecue, light at least 20 minutes before required. Strip the leaves from the rosemary stems, leaving about 5 cm/2 inches of soft leaves at the top. Chop the leaves coarsely and reserve. Using a sharp knife, cut the thicker woody ends of the stems to a point which can pierce the chicken pieces and potatoes. Blend the chopped rosemary, oil, garlic, thyme and lemon rind and juice in a shallow dish. Season to taste with salt and pepper.

2 Cut the chicken into 4 cm/ ½ inch cubes, add to the flavoured oil and stir well. Cover, refrigerate for at least 30 minutes, turning occasionally.

3 Cook the potatoes in lightly salted boiling water for 10–12 minutes until just tender.

Add the onions to the potatoes 2 minutes before the end of the cooking time. Drain, rinse under cold running water and leave to cool. Cut the pepper into 2.5 cm/ 1 inch squares.

4 Beginning with a piece of chicken and starting with the pointed end of the skewer, alternately thread equal amounts of chicken, potato, pepper and onion onto each rosemary skewer. Cover the leafy ends of the skewers with tinfoil to stop them from burning. Do not thread the chicken and vegetables too closely together on the skewer or the chicken may not cook completely.

5 Cook the kebabs for 15 minutes, or until tender and golden, turning and brushing with either extra oil or the marinade. Remove the tinfoil, garnish with lemon wedges and serve on rice.

AROMATIC CHICKEN CURRY

INGREDIENTS   Serves 4

125 g/4 oz red lentils
2 tsp ground coriander
½ tsp cumin seeds
2 tsp mild curry paste
1 bay leaf
small strip of lemon rind
600 ml/1 pint chicken or
   vegetable stock
8 chicken thighs, skinned
175 g/6 oz spinach leaves,
   rinsed and shredded

1 tbsp freshly
   chopped coriander
2 tsp lemon juice
salt and freshly ground
   black pepper

TO SERVE:
freshly cooked rice
low fat natural yogurt

1 Put the lentils in a sieve and rinse thoroughly under cold running water.

2 Dry-fry the ground coriander and cumin seeds in a large saucepan over a low heat for about 30 seconds. Stir in the curry paste.

3 Add the lentils to the saucepan with the bay leaf and lemon rind, then pour in the stock.

4 Stir, then slowly bring to the boil. Turn down the heat, half-cover the pan with a lid and simmer gently for 5 minutes, stirring occasionally.

5 Secure the chicken thighs with cocktail sticks to keep their shape. Place in the pan and half-cover. Simmer for 15 minutes.

6 Stir in the shredded spinach and cook for a further 25

minutes or until the chicken is very tender and the sauce is thick.

7 Remove the bay leaf and lemon rind. Stir in the coriander and lemon juice, then season to taste with salt and pepper. Serve immediately with the rice and a little natural yogurt.

HELPFUL HINT

Dry-frying spices really releases the flavour of the spices and is a technique that can be used in many dishes. It is a particularly good way to flavour lean meat or fish. Try mixing dry-fried spices with a little water or oil to make a paste. Spread the paste on meat or fish before baking to make a spicy crust.

164

CHICKEN PIE WITH SWEET POTATO TOPPING

INGREDIENTS — Serves 4

700 g/1½ lb sweet potatoes, peeled and cut into chunks
salt and freshly ground black pepper
250 g/9 oz potatoes, peeled and cut into chunks
150 ml/¼ pint milk
25 g/1 oz butter
2 tsp brown sugar
grated rind of 1 orange
4 skinless chicken breast fillets, diced

1 medium onion, peeled and coarsely chopped
125 g/4 oz baby mushrooms, stems trimmed
2 leeks, trimmed and thickly sliced
150 ml/¼ pint dry white wine
1 chicken stock cube
1 tbsp freshly chopped parsley
50 ml/2 fl oz crème fraîche or thick double cream
green vegetables, to serve

1 Preheat the oven to 190°C/375°F/Gas Mark 5, 10 minutes before required. Cook the potatoes in lightly salted boiling water until tender. Drain well, then return to the saucepan and mash until smooth and creamy, gradually adding the milk, then the butter, sugar and orange rind. Season to taste with salt and pepper and reserve.

2 Place the chicken in a saucepan with the onion, mushrooms, leeks, wine, stock cube and season to taste. Simmer, covered, until the chicken and vegetables are tender. Using a slotted spoon, transfer the chicken and vegetables to a 1.1 litre/2 pint pie dish. Add the parsley and crème fraîche or cream to the liquid in the pan and bring to the boil. Simmer until thickened and smooth, stirring constantly. Pour over the chicken in the pie dish, mix and cool.

3 Spread the mashed potato over the chicken filling, and swirl the surface into decorative peaks. Bake in the preheated oven for 35 minutes, or until the top is golden and the chicken filling is heated through. Serve immediately with fresh green vegetables.

HELPFUL HINT

There are 2 types of sweet potato; one has a creamy-coloured flesh, the other orange. Both are suitable for mashing as in this recipe, but the cream-coloured variety has a drier texture, so you may need a little more milk.

ORANGE ROASTED WHOLE CHICKEN

INGREDIENTS   Serves 6

1 small orange, thinly sliced
50 g/2 oz sugar
1.4 kg/3 lb oven-ready chicken
1 small bunch fresh coriander
1 small bunch fresh mint
2 tbsp olive oil
1 tsp Chinese five spice powder
½ tsp paprika

1 tsp fennel seeds, crushed
salt and freshly ground black
  pepper
sprigs of fresh coriander,
  to garnish
freshly cooked vegetables,
  to serve

1 Preheat the oven to 190°C/ 375°F/Gas Mark 5, 10 minutes before cooking. Place the orange slices in a small saucepan, cover with water, bring to the boil, then simmer for 2 minutes and drain. Place the sugar in a clean saucepan with 150 ml/¼ pint fresh water. Stir over a low heat until the sugar dissolves, then bring to the boil, add the drained orange slices and simmer for 10 minutes. Remove from the heat and leave in the syrup until cold.

2 Remove any excess fat from inside the chicken. Starting at the neck end, carefully loosen the skin of the chicken over the breast and legs without tearing. Push the orange slices under the loosened skin with the coriander and mint.

3 Mix together the olive oil, Chinese five spice powder, paprika and crushed fennel seeds and season to taste with salt and pepper. Brush the chicken skin

generously with this mixture. Transfer to a wire rack set over a roasting tin and roast in the preheated oven for 1½ hours, or until the juices run clear when a skewer is inserted into the thickest part of the thigh. Remove from the oven and leave to rest for 10 minutes. Garnish with sprigs of fresh coriander and serve with freshly cooked vegetables.

TASTY TIP

To make oven-baked rice, soften a chopped onion in 1 tablespoon sunflower oil in an ovenproof casserole. Stir in 250 g/9 oz long-grain rice, then remove from the heat. Pour in 750 ml/1¼ pints chicken or vegetable stock, 1 star anise, ½ cinnamon stick, 1 bay leaf, salt and pepper. Cover and cook for 45 minutes or until tender. Fluff up with a fork and remove the spices.

SLOW ROAST CHICKEN WITH POTATOES & OREGANO

INGREDIENTS   Serves 6

1.4–1.8 kg/3–4 lb oven-ready chicken, preferably free range
1 lemon, halved
1 onion, peeled and quartered
50 g/2 oz butter, softened
salt and freshly ground black pepper

1 kg/2¼ lb potatoes, peeled and quartered
3–4 tbsp extra-virgin olive oil
1 tbsp dried oregano, crumbled
1 tsp fresh thyme leaves
2 tbsp freshly chopped thyme
fresh sage leaves, to garnish

1 Preheat the oven to 200°C/400°F/Gas Mark 6. Rinse the chicken and dry well, inside and out, with absorbent kitchen paper. Rub the chicken all over with the lemon halves, then squeeze the juice over it and into the cavity. Put the squeezed halves into the cavity with the quartered onion.

2 Rub the softened butter all over the chicken and season to taste with salt and pepper, then put it in a large roasting tin, breast-side down.

3 Toss the potatoes in the oil, season with salt and pepper to taste and add the dried oregano and fresh thyme. Arrange the potatoes with the oil around the chicken and carefully pour 150 ml/¼ pint water into one end of the pan (not over the oil).

4 Roast in the preheated oven for 25 minutes. Reduce the oven temperature to 190°C/375°F/Gas Mark 5 and turn the chicken breast-side up. Turn the potatoes, sprinkle over half the fresh herbs and baste the chicken and potatoes with the juices. Continue roasting for 1 hour, or until the chicken is cooked, basting occasionally. If the liquid evaporates completely, add a little more water. The chicken is done when the juices run clear when the thigh is pierced with a skewer.

5 Transfer the chicken to a carving board and rest for 5 minutes, covered with tinfoil. Return the potatoes to the oven while the chicken is resting.

6 Carve the chicken into serving pieces and arrange on a large heatproof serving dish. Arrange the potatoes around the chicken and drizzle over any remaining juices. Sprinkle with the remaining herbs and serve.

TURKEY & PESTO RICE ROULADES

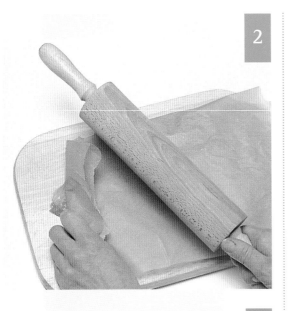

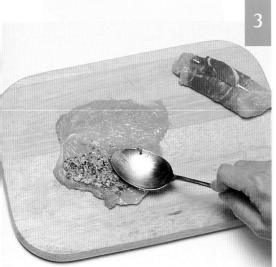

INGREDIENTS   Serves 4

125 g/4 oz cooked white rice, at room temperature

1 garlic clove, peeled and crushed

1–2 tbsp Parmesan cheese, grated

2 tbsp prepared pesto sauce

2 tbsp pine nuts, lightly toasted and chopped

4 turkey steaks, each weighing about 150 g/5 oz

salt and freshly ground black pepper

4 slices Parma ham

2 tbsp olive oil

50 ml/2 fl oz white wine

25 g/1 oz unsalted butter, chilled

TO SERVE:

freshly cooked spinach

freshly cooked pasta

1 Put the rice in a bowl and add the garlic, Parmesan cheese, pesto and pine nuts. Stir to combine the ingredients, then reserve.

2 Place the turkey steaks on a chopping board and, using a sharp knife, cut horizontally through each steak, without cutting right through. Open up the steaks and cover with baking parchment. Flatten slightly by pounding with a meat mallet or rolling pin.

3 Season each steak with salt and pepper. Divide the stuffing equally among the steaks, spreading evenly over one half. Fold the steaks in half to enclose the filling, then wrap each steak in a slice of Parma ham and secure with cocktail sticks.

4 Heat the oil in a large frying pan over medium heat. Cook the steaks for 5 minutes, or until golden on one side. Turn and cook for a further 2 minutes. Push the steaks to the side and pour in the wine. Allow the wine to bubble and evaporate. Add the butter, a little at a time, whisking constantly until the sauce is smooth. Discard the cocktail sticks, then serve the steaks drizzled with the sauce and serve with spinach and pasta.

FOOD FACT

The classic Italian Parma ham is dry-cured, whereby it is rubbed with salt for about a month, then hung up to dry for a year. Carved very thinly, it often served raw, but is also good when lightly fried.

HOISIN DUCK & GREENS STIR FRY

INGREDIENTS   Serves 4

350 g/12 oz duck breasts, skinned and cut into strips
1 medium egg white, beaten
½ tsp salt
1 tsp sesame oil
2 tsp cornflour
2 tbsp groundnut oil
2 tbsp freshly grated root ginger
50 g/2 oz bamboo shoots

50 g/2 oz fine green beans, trimmed
50 g/2 oz pak choi, trimmed
2 tbsp hoisin sauce
1 tsp Chinese rice wine or dry sherry
zest and juice of ½ orange
strips of orange zest, to garnish
freshly steamed egg noodles, to serve

1 Place the duck strips in a shallow dish, then add the egg white, salt, sesame oil and cornflour. Stir lightly until the duck is coated in the mixture. Cover and chill in the refrigerator for 20 minutes.

2 Heat the wok until very hot and add the oil. Remove the wok from the heat and add the duck, stirring continuously to prevent the duck from sticking to the wok. Add the ginger and stir-fry for 2 minutes. Add the bamboo shoots, the green beans and the pak choi, and stir-fry for 1–2 minutes until wilted.

3 Mix together the hoisin sauce, the Chinese rice wine or sherry and the orange zest and juice. Pour into the wok and stir to coat the duck and vegetables. Stir-fry for 1–2 minutes, or until

the duck and vegetables are tender. Garnish with the strips of orange zest and serve immediately with freshly steamed egg noodles.

HELPFUL HINT

Duck breasts are usually sold with the skin on, but it is very easy to remove and all the fat usually comes away readily with the skin. If any remains, simply remove with a sharp knife.

FRIED GINGER RICE WITH SOY GLAZED DUCK

INGREDIENTS   Serves 4–6

2 duck breasts, skinned and diagonally cut into thin slices

2–3 tbsp Japanese soy sauce

1 tbsp mirin (sweet rice wine) or sherry

2 tbsp brown sugar

5 cm/2 inch piece of fresh root ginger, peeled and finely chopped

4 tbsp peanut or vegetable oil

2 garlic cloves, peeled and crushed

300 g/11 oz long-grain brown rice

900 ml/1½ pints chicken stock

freshly ground black pepper

125 g/4 oz lean ham, diced

175 g/6 oz mangetout, diagonally cut in half

8 spring onions, trimmed and diagonally thinly sliced

1 tbsp freshly chopped coriander

sweet or hot chilli sauce, to taste (optional)

sprigs of fresh coriander, to garnish

1 Put the duck slices in a bowl with 1 tablespoon of the soy sauce, the mirin, 1 teaspoon of the sugar and one-third of the ginger; stir. Leave to stand.

2 Heat 2 tablespoons of the oil in a large heavy-based saucepan. Add the garlic and half the remaining ginger and stir-fry for 1 minute. Add the rice and cook for 3 minutes, stirring constantly, until translucent.

3 Stir in all but 125 ml/4 fl oz of the stock, with 1 teaspoon of the soy sauce, and bring to the boil. Season with pepper. Reduce the heat to very low and simmer, covered, for 25–30 minutes until the rice is tender and the liquid is absorbed. Cover and leave to stand.

4 Heat the remaining oil in a large frying pan or wok. Drain the duck strips and add to the frying pan. Stir-fry for 2–3 minutes until just coloured. Add 1 tablespoon of soy sauce and the remaining sugar and cook for 1 minute until glazed. Transfer to a plate and keep warm.

5 Stir in the ham, mangetout, spring onions, the remaining ginger and the chopped coriander. Add the remaining stock and duck marinade and cook until the liquid is almost reduced. Fork in the rice and a little chilli sauce to taste (if using); stir well. Turn into a serving dish and top with the duck. Garnish with coriander sprigs and serve immediately.

FUSILLI PASTA WITH SPICY TOMATO SALSA

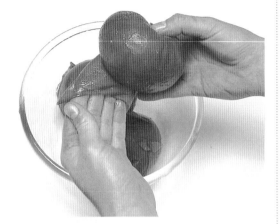

INGREDIENTS   Serves 4

6 large ripe tomatoes
2 tbsp lemon juice
2 tbsp lime juice
grated rind of 1 lime
2 shallots, peeled and
    finely chopped
2 garlic cloves, peeled
    and finely chopped

1–2 red chillies
1–2 green chillies
450 g/1 lb fresh fusilli pasta
4 tbsp half-fat crème fraîche
2 tbsp freshly chopped basil
sprig of oregano, to garnish

1 Place the tomatoes in a bowl and cover with boiling water. Allow to stand until the skins start to peel away.

2 Remove the skins from the tomatoes, divide each tomato in four and remove all the seeds. Chop the flesh into small dice and put in a small pan. Add the lemon and lime juice and the grated lime rind and stir well.

3 Add the chopped shallots and garlic. Remove the seeds carefully from the chillies, chop finely and add to the pan.

4 Bring to the boil and simmer gently for 5–10 minutes until the salsa has thickened slightly.

5 Reserve the salsa to allow the flavours to develop while the pasta is cooking.

6 Bring a large pan of water to the boil and add the pasta.

Simmer gently for 3–4 minutes or until the pasta is just tender.

7 Drain the pasta and rinse in boiling water. Top with a large spoonful of salsa and a small spoonful of crème fraîche. Garnish with the chopped basil and oregano and serve immediately.

FOOD FACT

Pasta is an excellent source of complex carbohydrate and is vital for a healthy lifestyle. Complex carbohydrates are broken down by the body more slowly than simple carbohydrates (contained in cakes, sweets and biscuits) and provide a sustained source of energy.

SINGAPORE NOODLES

INGREDIENTS   Serves 4

225 g/8 oz thin round egg
noodles

3 tbsp groundnut or vegetable
oil

125 g/4 oz field mushrooms,
wiped and thinly sliced

2.5 cm/1 inch piece root
ginger, peeled and finely
chopped

1 red chilli, deseeded and
thinly sliced

1 red pepper, deseeded and
thinly sliced

2 garlic cloves, peeled and
crushed

1 medium courgette, cut in
half lengthwise and
diagonally sliced

4-6 spring onions, trimmed
and thinly sliced

50 g/2 oz frozen garden peas,
thawed

1 tbsp curry paste

2 tbsp tomato ketchup

salt or soy sauce

125 g/4 oz beansprouts, rinsed
and drained

TO GARNISH:
sesame seeds
fresh coriander leaves

1 Bring a large pan of lightly salted water to a rolling boil. Add the noodles and cook according to the packet instructions, or until 'al dente'. Drain thoroughly and toss with 1 tablespoon of the oil.

2 Heat the remaining oil in a wok or large frying pan over high heat. Add the mushrooms, ginger, chilli and red pepper and stir-fry for 2 minutes. Add the garlic, courgettes, spring onions and garden peas and stir lightly.

3 Push the vegetables to one side and add the curry paste, tomato ketchup and about 125 ml/4 fl oz hot water. Season to taste with salt or a few drops of soy sauce and allow to boil

vigorously, stirring, until the paste is smooth.

4 Stir the reserved egg noodles and the beansprouts into the vegetable mixture and stir-fry until coated with the paste and thoroughly heated through. Season with more soy sauce if necessary, then turn into a large warmed serving bowl or spoon on to individual plates. Garnish with sesame seeds and coriander leaves. Serve immediately.

BEETROOT & POTATO MEDLEY

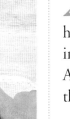

INGREDIENTS   Serves 4

350 g/12 oz raw
  baby beetroot
½ tsp sunflower oil
225 g/8 oz new potatoes
½ cucumber, peeled
3 tbsp white wine vinegar
150 ml/5 fl oz natural
  low-fat yogurt

salt and freshly ground
  black pepper
fresh salad leaves
1 tbsp freshly snipped chives,
  to garnish

1 Preheat the oven to 180°C/350°F/Gas Mark 4. Scrub the beetroot thoroughly and place on a baking tray.

2 Brush the beetroot with a little oil and cook for 1½ hours or until a skewer is easily insertable into the beetroot. Allow to cool a little, then remove the skins.

3 Cook the potatoes in boiling water for about 10 minutes. Rinse in cold water and drain. Reserve the potatoes until cool. Dice evenly.

4 Cut the cucumber into cubes and place in a mixing bowl. Chop the beetroot into small cubes and add to the bowl with the reserved potatoes. Gently mix the vegetables together.

5 Mix together the vinegar and yogurt and season to taste with a little salt and pepper. Pour over the vegetables and combine gently.

6 Arrange on a bed of salad leaves garnished with the snipped chives and serve.

HELPFUL HINT

Beetroot can also be cooked in the microwave. Place in a microwaveable bowl. Add sufficient water to come halfway up the sides of the bowl. Cover and cook for 10–15 minutes on high. Leave for 5 minutes before removing the paper. Cook before peeling.

FOOD FACT

Like other fruits and vegetables which are red in colour, beetroot has particularly high levels of antioxidants which are essential to the body to fight disease.

SWEET POTATO CAKES WITH MANGO & TOMATO SALSA

INGREDIENTS   Serves 4

700 g/1½ lb sweet potatoes, peeled and cut into large chunks

salt and freshly ground black pepper

25 g/1 oz butter

1 onion, peeled and chopped

1 garlic clove, peeled and crushed

pinch of freshly grated nutmeg

1 medium egg, beaten

50 g/2 oz quick-cook polenta

2 tbsp sunflower oil

FOR THE SALSA:

1 ripe mango, peeled, stoned and diced

6 cherry tomatoes, cut in wedges

4 spring onions, trimmed and thinly sliced

1 red chilli, deseeded and finely chopped

finely grated rind and juice of ½ lime

2 tbsp freshly chopped mint

1 tsp clear honey

salad leaves, to serve

1 Steam or cook the sweet potatoes in lightly salted boiling water for 15–20 minutes, until tender. Drain well, then mash until smooth.

2 Melt the butter in a saucepan. Add the onion and garlic and cook gently for 10 minutes until soft. Add to the mashed sweet potato and season with the nutmeg, salt and pepper. Stir together until mixed thoroughly. Leave to cool.

3 Shape the mixture into 4 oval potato cakes, about 2.5 cm/ 1 inch thick. Dip first in the beaten egg, allowing the excess to fall back into the bowl, then coat in the polenta. Refrigerate for at least 30 minutes.

4 Meanwhile, mix together all the ingredients for the salsa. Spoon into a serving bowl, cover with clingfilm and leave at room temperature to allow the flavours to develop.

5 Heat the oil in a frying pan and cook the potato cakes for 4–5 minutes on each side. Serve with the salsa and salad leaves.

FOOD FACT

Polenta is finely ground, golden cornmeal from Italy. It is often made into a soft, savoury mixture of the same name, but also makes an excellent coating for foods such as these potato cakes.

Sicilian Baked Aubergine

1

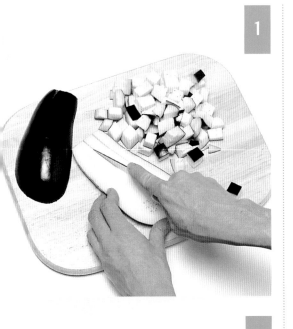

5

6

INGREDIENTS   Serves 4

1 large aubergine, trimmed
2 celery stalks, trimmed
4 large ripe tomatoes
1 tsp sunflower oil
2 shallots, peeled and
   finely chopped
1½ tsp tomato purée
25 g/1 oz green pitted olives

25 g/1 oz black pitted olives
salt and freshly ground
   black pepper
1 tbsp white wine vinegar
2 tsp caster sugar
1 tbsp freshly chopped basil,
   to garnish
mixed salad leaves, to serve

1 Preheat the oven to 200°C/ 400°F/Gas Mark 6. Cut the aubergine into small cubes and place on an oiled baking tray.

2 Cover the tray with tinfoil and bake in the preheated oven for 15–20 minutes until soft. Reserve, to allow the aubergine to cool.

3 Place the celery and tomatoes in a large bowl and cover with boiling water.

4 Remove the tomatoes from the bowl when their skins begin to peel away. Remove the skins then, deseed and chop the flesh into small pieces.

5 Remove the celery from the bowl of water, finely chop and reserve.

6 Pour the vegetable oil into a non-stick saucepan, add the chopped shallots and fry gently for 2–3 minutes until soft. Add the celery, tomatoes, tomato

purée and olives. Season to taste with salt and pepper.

7 Simmer gently for 3–4 minutes. Add the vinegar, sugar and cooled aubergine to the pan and heat gently for 2–3 minutes until all the ingredients are well blended. Reserve to allow the aubergine mixture to cool. When cool, garnish with the chopped basil and serve cold with salad leaves.

FOOD FACT

It has been suggested, that foods which are purple in colour, such as aubergines, have particularly powerful antioxidants, which help the body to protect itself from disease and strengthen the organs.

MIXED VEGETABLES STIR FRY

INGREDIENTS   Serves 4

2 tbsp groundnut oil

4 garlic cloves, peeled and finely sliced

2.5 cm/1 inch piece fresh root ginger, peeled and finely sliced

75 g/3 oz broccoli florets

50 g/2 oz mangetout, trimmed

75 g/3 oz carrots, peeled and cut into matchsticks

1 green pepper, deseeded and cut into strips

1 red pepper, deseeded and cut into strips

1 tbsp soy sauce

1 tbsp hoisin sauce

1 tsp sugar

salt and freshly ground black pepper

4 spring onions, trimmed and shredded, to garnish

1 Heat a wok, add the oil and when hot, add the garlic and ginger slices and stir-fry for 1 minute.

2 Add the broccoli florets to the wok, stir-fry for 1 minute, then add the mangetout, carrots and the green and red peppers and stir-fry for a further 3–4 minutes, or until tender but still crisp.

3 Blend the soy sauce, hoisin sauce and sugar in a small bowl. Stir well, season to taste with salt and pepper and pour into the wok. Transfer the vegetables to a warmed serving dish. Garnish with shredded spring onions and serve immediately with a selection of other Thai dishes.

FOOD FACT

Hoisin sauce is a thick, dark brownish red sauce, made by blending soya beans with sugar, vinegar and spices. It has a spicy, sweetish taste and is often used in southern Chinese cooking. It may also be served as a sauce for Peking duck instead of the more traditional sweet bean sauce.

HELPFUL HINT

Vary the combination of vegetables – try asparagus spears cut into short lengths, sliced mushroons, French beans, red onion wedges and cauliflower florets.

VEGETARIAN CASSOULET

INGREDIENTS   Serves 4

225 g/8 oz dried haricot beans, soaked overnight

2 medium onions

1 bay leaf

1.4 litres/2½ pints cold water

550 g/1¼ lb large potatoes, peeled and cut into 1 cm/ ½ inch slices

salt and freshly ground black pepper

5 tsp olive oil

1 large garlic clove, peeled and crushed

2 leeks, trimmed and sliced

200 g can chopped tomatoes

1 tsp dark muscovado sugar

1 tbsp freshly chopped thyme

2 tbsp freshly chopped parsley

3 courgettes, trimmed and sliced

FOR THE TOPPING:

50 g/2 oz fresh white breadcrumbs

25 g/1oz Cheddar cheese, finely grated

1 Preheat the oven to 180°C/ 350°F/Gas Mark 4, 10 minutes before required. Drain the beans, rinse under cold running water and put in a saucepan. Peel 1 of the onions and add to the beans with the bay leaf. Pour in the water.

2 Bring to a rapid boil and cook for 10 minutes, then turn down the heat, cover and simmer for 50 minutes, or until the beans are almost tender. Drain the beans, reserving the liquor, but discarding the onion and bay leaf.

3 Cook the potatoes in a saucepan of lightly salted boiling water for 6–7 minutes until almost tender when tested with the point of a knife. Drain and reserve.

4 Peel and chop the remaining onion. Heat the oil in a frying pan and cook the onion with the garlic and leeks for 10 minutes until softened. Stir in the tomatoes, sugar, thyme and parsley. Stir in the beans, with 300 ml/½ pint of the reserved liquor and season to taste. Simmer, uncovered, for 5 minutes.

5 Layer the potato slices, courgettes and ladlefuls of the bean mixture in a large flameproof casserole. To make the topping, mix together the breadcrumbs and cheese and sprinkle over the top.

6 Bake in the preheated oven for 40 minutes, or until the vegetables are cooked through and the topping is golden brown and crisp. Serve immediately.

CABBAGE TIMBALE

INGREDIENTS   Serves 4–6

1 small savoy cabbage,
  weighing about 350 g/12 oz
salt and freshly ground black
  pepper
2 tbsp olive oil
1 leek, trimmed and chopped
1 garlic clove, peeled and
  crushed
75 g/3 oz long-grain rice
200 g can chopped tomatoes

300 ml/½ pint vegetable stock
400 g can flageolet beans,
  drained and rinsed
75 g/3 oz Cheddar cheese,
  grated
1 tbsp freshly chopped oregano

TO GARNISH:
Greek yogurt with paprika
tomato wedges

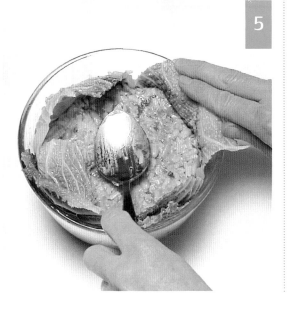

1 Preheat the oven to 180°C/ 350°F/Gas Mark 4, 10 minutes before required. Remove 6 of the outer leaves of the cabbage. Cut off the thickest part of the stalk and blanch the leaves in lightly salted boiling water for 2 minutes. Lift out with a slotted spoon and briefly rinse under cold water and reserve.

2 Remove the stalks from the rest of the cabbage leaves. Shred the leaves and blanch in the boiling water for 1 minute. Drain, rinse under cold water and pat dry on absorbent kitchen paper.

3 Heat the oil in a frying pan and cook the leek and garlic for 5 minutes. Stir in the rice, chopped tomatoes with their juice and stock. Bring to the boil, cover and simmer for 15 minutes.

4 Remove the lid and simmer for a further 4–5 minutes, stirring frequently, until the liquid is absorbed and the rice is tender. Stir in the flageolet beans, cheese and oregano. Season to taste with salt and pepper.

5 Line an oiled 1.1 litre/2 pint pudding basin with some of the large cabbage leaves, over-lapping them slightly. Fill the basin with alternate layers of rice mixture and shredded leaves, pressing down well.

6 Cover the top with the remaining leaves. Cover with oiled tinfoil and bake in the preheated for 30 minutes. Leave to stand for 10 minutes. Turn out, cut into wedges and serve with yogurt sprinkled with paprika and tomato wedges.

HANDY HINT

Avoid red or white cabbage
for this recipe as their leaves
are not flexible enough.

PASTA WITH RAW FENNEL, TOMATO & RED ONIONS

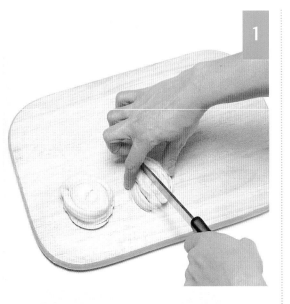

INGREDIENTS   Serves 6

1 fennel bulb
700 g/1½ lb tomatoes
1 garlic clove
¼ small red onion
small handful fresh basil
small handful fresh mint
100 ml/3½ fl oz extra virgin
  olive oil, plus extra to serve

juice of 1 lemon
salt and freshly ground black
  pepper
450 g/1 lb penne or pennette
freshly grated Parmesan
  cheese, to serve

1 Trim the fennel and slice thinly. Stack the slices and cut into sticks, then cut crosswise again into fine dice. De-seed the tomatoes and chop them finely. Peel and finely chop or crush the garlic. Peel and finely chop or grate the onion.

2 Stack the basil leaves then roll up tightly. Slice crosswise into fine shreds. Finely chop the mint.

3 Place the chopped vegetables and herbs in a medium bowl. Add the olive oil and lemon juice and mix together. Season well with salt and pepper then leave for 30 minutes to allow the flavours to develop.

4 Bring a large pan of salted water to a rolling boil. Add the pasta and cook according to the packet instructions, or until 'al dente'.

5 Drain the cooked pasta thoroughly. Transfer to a warmed serving dish, pour over the vegetable mixture and toss. Serve with the grated Parmesan cheese and extra olive oil to drizzle over.

TASTY TIP

Fennel is a greenish-white bulbous vegetable that has a distinctive aniseed flavour. It is also known as Florence fennel to distinguish it from the herb. When buying fennel, choose a bulb that is well-rounded and as white as possible; the darker green ones may be bitter. Trim off the feathery leaves, chop them finely and use as a garnish.

RED LENTIL KEDGEREE WITH AVOCADO & TOMATOES

INGREDIENTS   Serves 4

150 g/5 oz basmati rice
150 g/5 oz red lentils
15 g/½ oz butter
1 tbsp sunflower oil
1 medium onion, peeled and
  chopped
1 tsp ground cumin
4 cardamom pods, bruised
1 bay leaf
450 ml/¾ pint vegetable stock
1 ripe avocado, peeled, stoned
  and diced

1 tbsp lemon juice
4 plum tomatoes, peeled and
  diced
2 tbsp freshly chopped
  coriander
salt and freshly ground black
  pepper
lemon or lime slices, to
  garnish

1 Put the rice and lentils in a sieve and rinse under cold running water. Tip into a bowl, then pour over enough cold water to cover and leave to soak for 10 minutes.

2 Heat the butter and oil in a saucepan. Add the sliced onion and cook gently, stirring occasionally, for 10 minutes until softened. Stir in the cumin, cardamon pods and bay leaf and cook for a further minute, stirring all the time.

3 Drain the rice and lentils, rinse again and add to the onions in the saucepan. Stir in the vegetable stock and bring to the boil. Reduce the heat, cover the saucepan and simmer for 14–15 minutes, or until the rice and lentils are tender.

4 Place the diced avocado in a bowl and toss with the lemon juice. Stir in the tomatoes and chopped coriander. Season to taste with salt and pepper.

5 Fluff up the rice with a fork, spoon into a warmed serving dish and spoon the avocado mixture on top. Garnish with lemon or lime slices and serve.

TASTY TIP

Although basmati rice and red lentils do not usually need to be pre-soaked, it improves the results of this recipe: the rice will cook to very light, fluffy separate grains and the lentils will just begin to break down giving the dish a creamier texture.

ADUKI BEAN & RICE BURGERS

INGREDIENTS   Serves 4

2½ tbsp sunflower oil
1 medium onion, peeled and
  very finely chopped
1 garlic clove, peeled and
  crushed
1 tsp curry paste
225 g/8 oz basmati rice
400 g can aduki beans,
  drained and rinsed
225 ml/8 fl oz vegetable stock
125 g/4 oz firm tofu, crumbled
1 tsp garam masala
2 tbsp freshly chopped
  coriander

salt and freshly ground black
  pepper

FOR THE CARROT RAITA:
2 large carrots, peeled and
  grated
½ cucumber, cut into tiny dice
150 ml/¼ pint Greek yogurt

TO SERVE:
wholemeal baps
tomato slices
lettuce leaves

1 Heat 1 tablespoon of the oil in a saucepan and gently cook the onion for 10 minutes until soft. Add the garlic and curry paste and cook for a few more seconds. Stir in the rice and beans.

2 Pour in the stock, bring to the boil and simmer for 12 minutes, or until all the stock has been absorbed – do not lift the lid for the first 10 minutes of cooking. Reserve.

3 Lightly mash the tofu. Add to the rice mixture with the garam masala, coriander, salt and pepper. Mix.

4 Divide the mixture into 8 and shape into burgers. Chill in the refrigerator for 30 minutes.

5 Meanwhile, make the raita. Mix together the carrots, cucumber and Greek yogurt. Spoon into a small bowl and chill in the refrigerator until ready to serve.

6 Heat the remaining oil in a large frying pan. Fry the burgers, in batches if necessary, for 4–5 minutes on each side, or until lightly browned. Serve in the baps with tomato slices and lettuce. Accompany with the raita.

FOOD FACT

Firm tofu is sold in blocks. It is made in a similar way to soft cheese and is the pressed curds of soya milk.

VEGETABLES BRAISED IN OLIVE OIL & LEMON

INGREDIENTS   Serves 4

small strip of pared rind and
juice of ½ lemon
4 tbsp olive oil
1 bay leaf
large sprig of thyme
150 ml/¼ pint water
4 spring onions, trimmed and
finely chopped
175 g/6 oz baby button
mushrooms

175 g/6 oz broccoli, cut into
small florets
175 g/6 oz cauliflower, cut into
small florets
1 medium courgette, sliced on
the diagonal
2 tbsp freshly snipped chives
salt and freshly ground black
pepper
lemon zest, to garnish

1 Put the pared lemon rind and juice into a large saucepan. Add the olive oil, bay leaf, thyme and the water. Bring to the boil. Add the spring onions and mushrooms. Top with the broccoli and cauliflower, trying to add them so that the stalks are submerged in the water and the tops are just above it. Cover and simmer for 3 minutes.

2 Scatter the courgettes on top, so that they are steamed rather than boiled. Cook, covered, for a further 3–4 minutes, until all the vegetables are tender. Using a slotted spoon, transfer the vegetables from the liquid into a warmed serving dish. Increase the heat and boil rapidly for 3–4 minutes, or until the liquid is reduced to about 8 tablespoons. Remove the lemon rind, bay leaf and thyme sprig and discard.

3 Stir the chives into the reduced liquid, season to taste with salt and pepper and pour over the vegetables. Sprinkle with lemon zest and serve immediately.

FOOD FACT

Serve these vegetables as an accompaniment to roasted or grilled chicken, fish or turkey. Alternatively, toast some crusty bread, rub with a garlic clove and drizzle with a little olive oil and top with a spoonful of vegetables.

MIXED GRAIN PILAF

INGREDIENTS   Serves 4

2 tbsp olive oil
1 garlic clove, peeled and
   crushed
½ tsp ground turmeric
125 g/4 oz mixed long-grain
   and wild rice
50 g/2 oz red lentils
300 ml/½ pint vegetable stock
200 g can chopped tomatoes
5 cm/2 inch piece cinnamon
   stick

salt and freshly ground black
   pepper
400 g can mixed beans,
   drained and rinsed
15 g/½ oz butter
1 bunch spring onions,
   trimmed and finely sliced
3 medium eggs
4 tbsp freshly chopped herbs,
   such as parsley and chervil
sprigs of fresh dill, to garnish

1 Heat 1 tablespoon of the oil in a saucepan. Add the garlic and turmeric and cook for a few seconds. Stir in the rice and lentils.

2 Add the stock, tomatoes and cinnamon. Season to taste with salt and pepper. Stir once and bring to the boil. Lower the heat, cover and simmer for 20 minutes, until most of the stock is absorbed and the rice and lentils are tender.

3 Stir in the beans, replace the lid and leave to stand for 2–3 minutes to allow the beans to heat through.

4 While the rice is cooking, heat the remaining oil and butter in a frying pan. Add the spring onions and cook for 4–5 minutes, until soft. Lightly beat the eggs with 2 tablespoons of the herbs, then season with salt and pepper.

5 Pour the egg mixture over the spring onions. Stir gently with a spatula over a low heat, drawing the mixture from the sides to the centre as the omelette sets. When almost set, stop stirring and cook for about 30 seconds until golden underneath.

6 Remove the omelette from the pan, roll up and slice into thin strips. Fluff the rice up with a fork and remove the cinnamon stick. Spoon onto serving plates, top with strips of omelette and the remaining chopped herbs. Garnish with sprigs of dill and serve.

HELPFUL HINT

Long-grain rice and wild rice have different cooking times, but in ready-mixed packets, the rice has been treated to even out the cooking times, making preparation simpler.

WILD RICE DOLMADES

INGREDIENTS Serves 4–6

6 tbsp olive oil
25 g/1 oz pine nuts
175 g/6 oz mushrooms, wiped
and finely chopped
4 spring onions, trimmed and
finely chopped
1 garlic clove, peeled and
crushed
50 g/2 oz cooked wild rice
2 tsp freshly chopped dill
2 tsp freshly chopped mint

salt and freshly ground black
pepper
16–24 prepared medium vine
leaves
about 300 ml/½ pint vegetable
stock

TO GARNISH:
lemon wedges
sprigs of fresh dill

1 Heat 1 tbsp of the oil in a frying pan and gently cook the pine nuts for 2–3 minutes, stirring frequently, until golden. Remove from the pan and reserve.

2 Add 1½ tablespoons of oil to the pan and gently cook the mushrooms, spring onions and garlic for 7–8 minutes until very soft. Stir in the rice, herbs, salt and pepper.

3 Put a heaped teaspoon of stuffing in the centre of each leaf (if the leaves are small, put 2 together, overlapping slightly). Fold over the stalk end, then the sides and roll up to make a neat parcel. Continue until all the stuffing is used.

4 Arrange the stuffed vine leaves close together seam-side down in a large saucepan, drizzling each with a little of the remaining oil – there will be several layers. Pour over just enough stock to cover.

5 Put an inverted plate over the dolmades to stop them unrolling during cooking. Bring to the boil, then simmer very gently for 3 minutes. Cool in the saucepan.

6 Transfer the dolmades to a serving dish. Cover and chill in the refrigerator before serving. Sprinkle with the pine nuts and garnish with lemon and dill. Serve.

HELPFUL HINT

Fresh vine leaves are available in early summer and should be blanched for 2–3 minutes in boiling water. Vine leaves preserved in brine can be found all year round in supermarkets – soak in warm water for 20 minutes before using.

HOT GRILLED CHICORY & PEARS

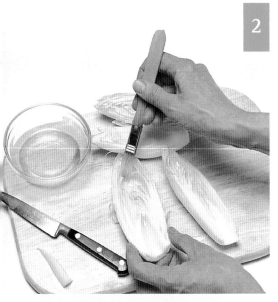

INGREDIENTS	Serves 4

50 g/2 oz unblanched almonds, roughly chopped
4 small heads of chicory
2 tbsp olive oil
1 tbsp walnut oil
2 firm ripe dessert pears
2 tsp lemon juice
1 tsp freshly chopped oregano

salt and freshly ground black pepper
freshly chopped oregano, to garnish
warmed ciabatta bread, to serve

1 Preheat grill. Spread the chopped almonds in a single layer on the grill pan. Cook under a hot grill for about 3 minutes, moving the almonds around occasionally, until lightly browned. Reserve.

2 Halve the chicory lengthways and cut out the cores. Mix together the olive and walnut oils. Brush about 2 tablespoons all over the chicory.

3 Put the chicory in a grill pan, cut-side up and cook under a hot grill for 2–3 minutes, or until beginning to char. Turn and cook for a further 1–2 minutes, then turn again.

4 Peel, core and thickly slice the pears. Brush with 1 tablespoon of the oils, then place the pears on top of the chicory. Grill for a further 3–4 minutes, or until both the chicory and pears are soft.

5 Transfer the chicory and pears to 4 warmed serving plates. Whisk together the remaining oil, lemon juice and oregano and season to taste with salt and pepper.

6 Drizzle the dressing over the chicory and pears and scatter with the toasted almonds. Garnish with fresh oregano and serve with ciabatta bread.

HELPFUL HINT

If preparing the pears ahead of time for this recipe, dip or brush them with some lemon juice to ensure that they do not discolour before cooking.

CHARGRILLED VEGETABLE & GOATS' CHEESE PIZZA

INGREDIENTS   Serves 4

125 g/4 oz baking potato
1 tbsp olive oil
225 g/8 oz strong white flour
½ tsp salt
1 tsp easy-blend dried yeast

FOR THE TOPPING:
1 medium aubergine, thinly
 sliced
2 small courgettes, trimmed
 and sliced lengthways
1 yellow pepper, quartered
 and deseeded

1 red onion, peeled and sliced
 into very thin wedges
5 tbsp olive oil
175 g/6 oz cooked new
 potatoes, halved
400 g can chopped tomatoes,
 drained
2 tsp freshly chopped oregano
125 g/4 oz mozzarella cheese,
 cut into small cubes
125 g/4 oz goats' cheese,
 crumbled

1 Preheat the oven to 220°C/
425°F/Gas Mark 7, 15
minutes before baking. Put a
baking sheet in the oven to heat
up. Cook the potato in lightly
salted boiling water until tender.
Peel and mash with the olive oil
until smooth.

2 Sift the flour and salt into a
bowl. Stir in the yeast. Add
the mashed potato and 150 ml/
¼ pint warm water and mix to
a soft dough. Knead for 5–6
minutes, until smooth. Put the
dough in a bowl, cover with
clingfilm and leave to rise in a
warm place for 30 minutes.

3 To make the topping, arrange
the aubergine, courgettes,
pepper and onion, skin-side up,
on a grill rack and brush with

4 tablespoons of the oil. Grill for
4–5 minutes. Turn the vegetables
and brush with the remaining oil.
Grill for 3–4 minutes. Cool, skin
and slice the pepper. Put all of
the vegetables in a bowl, add the
halved new potatoes and toss
gently together. Set aside.

4 Briefly re-knead the
dough then roll out to
a 30.5–35.5 cm/12–14 inch
round, according to preferred
thickness. Mix the tomatoes and
oregano together and spread over
the pizza base. Scatter over the
mozzarella cheese. Put the pizza
on the preheated baking sheet
and bake for 8 minutes.

5 Arrange the vegetables and
goats' cheese on top and bake
for 8–10 minutes. Serve.

COOKED VEGETABLE SALAD WITH SATAY SAUCE

INGREDIENTS   Serves 4

125 ml/4 fl oz groundnut oil
225 g/8 oz unsalted peanuts
1 onion, peeled and finely chopped
1 garlic clove, peeled and crushed
½ tsp chilli powder
1 tsp ground coriander
½ tsp ground cumin
½ tsp sugar
1 tbsp dark soy sauce
2 tbsp fresh lemon juice
2 tbsp light olive oil
salt and freshly ground black pepper

125 g/4 oz French green beans, trimmed and halved
125 g/4 oz carrots
125 g/4 oz cauliflower florets
125 g/4 oz broccoli florets
125 g/4 oz Chinese leaves or pak choi, trimmed and shredded
125 g/4 oz beansprouts
1 tbsp sesame oil

TO GARNISH:

sprigs of fresh watercress
cucumber, cut into slivers

1 Heat a wok, add the oil, and when hot, add the peanuts and stir-fry for 3–4 minutes. Drain on absorbent kitchen paper and leave to cool. Blend in a food processor to a fine powder.

2 Place the onion and garlic, with the spices, sugar, soy sauce, lemon juice and olive oil in a food processor. Season to taste with salt and pepper, then process into a paste. Transfer to a wok and stir-fry for 3–4 minutes.

3 Stir 600 ml/1 pint hot water into the paste and bring to the boil. Add the ground peanuts and simmer gently for 5–6 minutes or until the mixture thickens. Reserve the satay sauce.

4 Cook in batches in lightly salted boiling water. Cook the French beans, carrots, cauliflower and broccoli for 3–4 minutes, and the Chinese leaves or pak choi and beansprouts for 2 minutes. Drain each batch, drizzle over the sesame oil and arrange on a large warmed serving dish. Garnish with watercress sprigs and cucumber. Serve with the satay sauce.

FOOD FACT

Peanuts are not actually nuts, but a member of the pea family that grow underground. They are highly nutritious.

BABY ROAST POTATO SALAD

INGREDIENTS   Serves 4

350 g/12 oz small shallots
sea salt and freshly ground
   black pepper
900 g/2 lb small even-sized
   new potatoes
2 tbsp olive oil
2 medium courgettes

2 sprigs of fresh rosemary
175 g/6 oz cherry tomatoes
150 ml/¼ pint soured cream
2 tbsp freshly snipped chives
¼ tsp paprika

1 Preheat the oven to 200°C/ 400°F/Gas Mark 6. Trim the shallots, but leave the skins on. Put in a saucepan of lightly salted boiling water with the potatoes and cook for 5 minutes; drain. Separate the shallots and plunge them into cold water for 1 minute.

2 Put the oil in a baking sheet lined with tinfoil or roasting tin and heat for a few minutes. Peel the skins off the shallots – they should now come away easily. Add to the baking sheet or roasting tin with the potatoes and toss in the oil to coat. Sprinkle with a little sea salt. Roast the potatoes and shallots in the preheated oven for 10 minutes.

3 Meanwhile, trim the courgettes, halve lengthways and cut into 5 cm/2 inch chunks. Add to the baking sheet or roasting tin, toss to mix and cook for 5 minutes.

4 Pierce the tomato skins with a sharp knife. Add to the

sheet or tin with the rosemary and cook for a further 5 minutes, or until all the vegetables are tender. Remove the rosemary and discard. Grind a little black pepper over the vegetables.

5 Spoon into a wide serving bowl. Mix together the soured cream and chives and drizzle over the vegetables just before serving.

TASTY TIP

For a more substantial salad or to serve 6 rather than 4 people, add 225 g/8 oz baby aubergines, cut in half lengthways and cook with the potatoes and shallots, along with an extra 1 tablespoon olive oil. If you prefer, crème fraîche or Greek-style yogurt may be used instead of the soured cream.

MEDITERRANEAN RICE SALAD

INGREDIENTS   Serves 4

250 g/9 oz Camargue red rice
2 sun-dried tomatoes, finely
  chopped
2 garlic cloves, peeled and
  finely chopped
4 tbsp oil from a jar of sun-
  dried tomatoes
2 tsp balsamic vinegar
2 tsp red wine vinegar
salt and freshly ground black
  pepper
1 red onion, peeled and thinly
  sliced

1 yellow pepper, quartered
  and deseeded
1 red pepper, quartered and
  deseeded
½ cucumber, peeled and diced
6 ripe plum tomatoes, cut into
  wedges
1 fennel bulb, halved and
  thinly sliced
fresh basil leaves, to garnish

1 Cook the rice in a saucepan of lightly salted boiling water for 35–40 minutes, or until tender. Drain well and reserve.

2 Whisk the sun-dried tomatoes, garlic, oil and vinegars together in a small bowl or jug. Season to taste with salt and pepper. Put the red onion in a large bowl, pour over the dressing and leave to allow the flavours to develop.

3 Put the peppers, skin-side up on a grill rack and cook under a preheated hot grill for 5–6 minutes, or until blackened and charred. Remove and place in a plastic bag. When cool enough to handle, peel off the skins and slice the peppers.

4 Add the peppers, cucumber, tomatoes, fennel and rice to

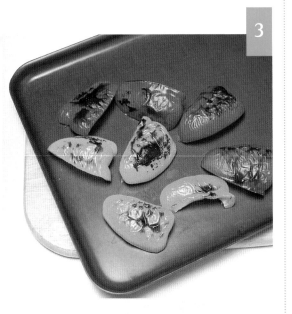

the onions. Mix gently together to coat in the dressing. Cover and chill in the refrigerator for 30 minutes to allow the flavours to mingle.

5 Remove the salad from the refrigerator and leave to stand at room temperature for 20 minutes. Garnish with fresh basil leaves and serve.

FOOD FACT

Camargue red rice from the south of France is a reddish-brown colour and gives this salad a stunning appearance. It has a texture and cooking time similar to that of brown rice, which may be substituted in this recipe if Camargue red rice is unavailable.

RICE & PAPAYA SALAD

INGREDIENTS   Serves 4

175 g/6 oz easy-cook basmati rice
1 cinnamon stick, bruised
1 bird's-eye chilli, deseeded and finely chopped
rind and juice of 2 limes
rind and juice of 2 lemons
2 tbsp Thai fish sauce
1 tbsp soft light brown sugar
1 papaya, peeled and seeds removed

1 mango, peeled and stone removed
1 green chilli, deseeded and finely chopped
2 tbsp freshly chopped coriander
1 tbsp freshly chopped mint
250 g/9 oz cooked chicken
50 g/2 oz roasted peanuts, chopped
strips of pitta bread, to serve

1 Rinse and drain the rice and pour into a saucepan. Add 450 ml/¾ pint boiling salted water and the cinnamon stick. Bring to the boil, reduce the heat to a very low heat, cover and cook without stirring for 15–18 minutes, or until all the liquid is absorbed. The rice should be light and fluffy and have steam holes on the surface. Remove the cinnamon stick and stir in the rind from 1 lime.

2 To make the dressing, place the bird's-eye chilli, remaining rind and lime and lemon juice, fish sauce and sugar in a food processor, mix for a few minutes until blended. Alternatively, place all these ingredients in a screw-top jar and shake until well blended. Pour half the dressing over the hot rice and toss until the rice glistens.

3 Slice the papaya and mango into thin slices, then place in a bowl. Add the chopped green chilli, coriander and mint. Place the chicken on a chopping board, then remove and discard any skin or sinews. Cut into fine shreds and add to the bowl with the chopped peanuts.

4 Add the remaining dressing to the chicken mixture and stir until all the ingredients are lightly coated. Spoon the rice onto a platter, pile the chicken mixture on top and serve with warm strips of pitta bread.

HELPFUL HINT

The papaya or pawpaw's skin turns from green when unripe, through to yellow and orange. To prepare, cut in half lengthways, scoop out the black seeds with a teaspoon and discard. Cut away the thin skin before slicing.

RICE WITH SMOKED SALMON & GINGER

INGREDIENTS   Serves 4

225 g/8 oz basmati rice
600 ml/1 pint fish stock
1 bunch spring onions,
   trimmed and diagonally
   sliced
3 tbsp freshly chopped
   coriander
1 tsp grated fresh root ginger

200 g/7 oz sliced smoked
   salmon
2 tbsp soy sauce
1 tsp sesame oil
2 tsp lemon juice
4–6 slices pickled ginger
2 tsp sesame seeds
rocket leaves, to serve

1 Place the rice in a sieve and rinse under cold water until the water runs clear. Drain, then place in a large saucepan with the stock and bring gently to the boil. Reduce to a simmer and cover with a tight-fitting lid. Cook for 10 minutes, then remove from the heat and leave, covered, for a further 10 minutes.

2 Stir the spring onions, coriander and fresh ginger into the cooked rice and mix well.

3 Spoon the rice into 4 tartlet tins, each measuring 10 cm/ 4 inches, and press down firmly with the back of a spoon to form cakes. Invert a tin onto an individual serving plate, then tap the base firmly and remove the tin. Repeat with the rest of the filled tins.

4 Top the rice with the salmon, folding if necessary, so the

sides of the rice can still be seen in places. Mix together the soy sauce, sesame oil and lemon juice to make a dressing, then drizzle over the salmon. Top with the pickled ginger and a sprinkling of sesame seeds. Scatter the rocket leaves around the edge of the plates and serve immediately.

FOOD FACT

Good smoked salmon should look moist and firm and have a peachy pink colour. If you buy it from a delicatessan counter, ask for it to be freshly sliced as any that has already been sliced may be dried out. Vacuum-packed salmon will keep for about 2 weeks in the refrigerator (check the use-by date), but once opened should be used within 3 days.

SALMON & FILO PARCELS

INGREDIENTS   Serves 4

1 tbsp sunflower oil
1 bunch of spring onions,
   trimmed and finely chopped
1 tsp paprika
175 g/6 oz long-grain white
   rice
300 ml/½ pint fish stock
salt and freshly ground black
   pepper

450 g/1 lb salmon fillet, cubed
1 tbsp freshly chopped parsley
grated rind and juice of 1
   lemon
150 g/5 oz rocket
150 g/5 oz spinach
12 sheets filo pastry
50 g/2 oz butter, melted

1 Preheat the oven to 200°C/ 400°F/Gas Mark 6. Heat the oil in a small frying pan and gently cook the spring onions for 2 minutes. Stir in the paprika and continue to cook for 1 minute, then remove from the heat and reserve.

2 Put the rice in a sieve and rinse under cold running water until the water runs clear; drain. Put the rice and stock in a saucepan, bring to the boil, then cover and simmer for 10 minutes, or until the liquid is absorbed and the rice is tender. Add the spring onion mixture and fork through. Season to taste with salt and pepper, then leave to cool.

3 In a non-metallic bowl, mix together the salmon, parsley, lemon rind and juice and salt and pepper. Reserve.

4 Blanch the rocket and spinach for 30 seconds in a large saucepan of boiling water, or until just wilted. Drain well in a colander and refresh in plenty of cold water, then squeeze out as much moisture as possible.

4 Brush 3 sheets of filo pastry with melted butter and lay them on top of one another. Take a quarter of the rice mixture and arrange it in an oblong in the centre of the pastry. On top of this place a quarter of the salmon followed by a quarter of the rocket and spinach.

5 Draw up the pastry around the filling and twist at the top to create a parcel. Repeat with the remaining pastry and filling until you have 4 parcels. Brush with the remaining butter.

6 Place the parcels on a lightly oiled baking tray and cook in the preheated oven for 20 minutes, or until golden brown and cooked. Serve immediately.

SALMON WITH HERBED POTATOES

2

INGREDIENTS · Serves 4

450 g/1 lb baby new potatoes
salt and freshly ground black
  pepper
4 salmon steaks, each
  weighing about 175 g/6 oz
1 carrot, peeled and cut into
  fine strips
175 g/6 oz asparagus spears,
  trimmed

175 g/6 oz sugar snap peas,
  trimmed
finely grated rind and juice 1
  lemon
25 g/1 oz butter
4 large sprigs of fresh parsley

3

1 Preheat the oven to 190°C/ 375°F/Gas Mark 5, about 10 minutes before required. Parboil the potatoes in lightly salted boiling water for 5–8 minutes until they are barely tender. Drain and reserve.

2 Cut out 4 pieces of baking parchment paper, measuring 20.5 cm/8 inches square, and place on the work surface. Arrange the parboiled potatoes on top. Wipe the salmon steaks and place on top of the potatoes.

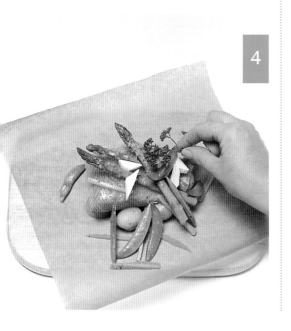

4

3 Place the carrot strips in a bowl with the asparagus spears, sugar snaps and grated lemon rind and juice. Season to taste with salt and pepper. Toss lightly together.

4 Divide the vegetables evenly between the salmon. Dot the top of each parcel with butter and a sprig of parsley.

5 To wrap a parcel, lift up 2 opposite sides of the paper and fold the edges together. Twist the paper at the other 2 ends to seal the parcel well. Repeat with the remaining parcels.

6 Place the parcels on a baking tray and bake in the preheated oven for 15 minutes. Place an unopened parcel on each plate and open just before eating.

HELPFUL HINT

Cooking fish *en papillote* is an excellent way of keeping in all the juices, flavour and aroma of the fish and vegetables. Your guests will also enjoy the anticipation of opening these surprise packages. Do let the parcels stand for a few minutes before serving as the steam can be burning hot when opened.

SALMON TERIYAKI WITH NOODLES & CRISPY GREENS

1

INGREDIENTS   Serves 4

350 g/12 oz salmon fillet
3 tbsp Japanese soy sauce
3 tbsp mirin or sweet sherry
3 tbsp sake
1 tbsp freshly grated root ginger
225 g/8 oz spring greens
groundnut oil for deep-frying
pinch of salt
½ tsp caster sugar
125 g/4 oz cellophane noodles

TO GARNISH:
1 tbsp freshly chopped dill
sprigs of fresh dill
zest of ½ lemon

2

6

1 Cut the salmon into paper-thin slices and place in a shallow dish. Mix together the soy sauce, mirin or sherry, sake and the ginger. Pour over the salmon, cover and leave to marinate for 15–30 minutes.

2 Remove and discard the thick stalks from the spring greens. Lay several leaves on top of each other, roll up tightly, then shred finely.

3 Pour in enough oil to cover about 5 cm/2 inches of the wok. Deep-fry the greens in batches for about 1 minute each until crisp. Remove and drain on absorbent kitchen paper. Transfer to a serving dish, sprinkle with salt and sugar and toss together.

4 Place the noodles in a bowl and pour over warm water to cover. Leave to soak for 15–20 minutes until soft, then drain. With scissors cut into 15 cm/ 6 inch lengths.

5 Preheat the grill. Remove the salmon slices from the marinade, reserving the marinade for later, and arrange them in a single layer on a baking sheet. Grill for about 2 minutes, until lightly cooked, without turning.

6 When the oil in the wok is cool enough, tip most of it away, leaving about 1 tablespoon behind. Heat until hot, then add the noodles and the reserved marinade and stir-fry for 3–4 minutes. Tip the noodles into a large warmed serving bowl and arrange the salmon slices on top, garnished with chopped dill, sprigs of fresh dill and lemon zest. Scatter with a little of the crispy greens and serve the rest separately.

SPAGHETTI ALLA PUTTANESCA

INGREDIENTS   Serves 4

4 tbsp olive oil
50 g/2 oz anchovy fillets in
  olive oil, drained and
  coarsely chopped
2 garlic cloves, peeled and
  finely chopped
½ tsp crushed dried chillies
400 g can chopped plum
  tomatoes
125 g/4 oz pitted black olives,
  cut in half

2 tbsp capers, rinsed and
  drained
1 tsp freshly chopped oregano
1 tbsp tomato paste
salt and freshly ground black
  pepper
400 g/14 oz spaghetti
2 tbsp freshly chopped parsley

1 Heat the olive oil in a large frying pan, add the anchovies and cook, stirring with a wooden spoon and crushing the anchovies, until they disintegrate. Add the garlic and dried chillies and cook for 1 minute, stirring frequently.

2 Add the tomatoes, olives, capers, oregano and tomato paste and cook, stirring occasionally, for 15 minutes, or until the liquid has evaporated and the sauce is thickened. Season the tomato sauce to taste with salt and pepper.

3 Meanwhile, bring a large pan of lightly salted water to a rolling boil. Add the spaghetti and cook according to the packet instructions, or until 'al dente'.

4 Drain the spaghetti thoroughly, reserving 1–2 tablespoons of the the cooking water. Return the spaghetti

with the reserved water to the pan. Pour the tomato sauce over the spaghetti, add the chopped parsley and toss to coat. Tip into a warmed serving dish or spoon on to individual plates and serve immediately.

TASTY TIP

Anchovies are mature sardines. They are heavily salted after filleting to preserve them, so should only be used in small quantities. For a less salty dish, drain them and soak in a little milk for about 20 minutes before using. You can, of course, omit the anchovies to make a vegetarian version of this recipe.

SWEET & SOUR RICE WITH CHICKEN

2

INGREDIENTS   Serves 4

4 spring onions
2 tsp sesame oil
1 tsp Chinese five spice powder
450 g/1 lb chicken breast, cut into cubes
1 tbsp oil
1 garlic clove, peeled and crushed
1 medium onion, peeled and sliced into thin wedges

225 g/8 oz long-grain white rice
600 ml/1 pint water
4 tbsp tomato ketchup
1 tbsp tomato purée
2 tbsp honey
1 tbsp vinegar
1 tbsp dark soy sauce
1 carrot, peeled and cut into matchsticks

3

1 Trim the spring onions, then cut lengthways into fine strips. Drop into a large bowl of iced water and reserve.

2 Mix together the sesame oil and Chinese five spice powder and use to rub into the cubed chicken. Heat the wok, then add the oil and when hot, cook the garlic and onion for 2–3 minutes, or until transparent and softened.

4

3 Add the chicken and stir-fry over a medium-high heat until the chicken is golden and cooked through. Using a slotted spoon, remove from the wok and keep warm.

4 Stir the rice into the wok and add the water, tomato ketchup, tomato purée, honey, vinegar and soy sauce. Stir well to mix. Bring to the boil, then simmer until almost all of the liquid is absorbed. Stir in the carrot and reserved chicken and continue to cook for 3–4 minutes.

5 Drain the spring onions, which will have become curly. Garnish with the spring onion curls and serve immediately with the rice and chicken.

FOOD FACT

Five-spice powder is a popular Chinese seasoning that can be bought ready-blended in jars in most supermarkets. It is a mixture of finely ground star anise, fennel, cinnamon, cloves and Sichuan pepper and adds a unique sweet and spicy aniseed flavour to food.

HERBED HASSELBACK POTATOES WITH ROAST CHICKEN

INGREDIENTS

Serves 4

8 medium, evenly-sized potatoes, peeled

3 large sprigs of fresh rosemary

1 tbsp oil

salt and freshly ground black pepper

350 g/12 oz baby parsnips, peeled

350 g/12 oz baby carrots, peeled

350 g/12 oz baby leeks, trimmed

75 g/3 oz butter

finely grated rind of 1 lemon, preferably unwaxed

1.6 kg/3½ lb chicken

1 Preheat the oven to 200°C/ 400°F/Gas Mark 6, about 15 minutes before cooking. Place a chopstick on either side of a potato and, with a sharp knife, cut down through the potato until you reach the chopsticks; take care not to cut right through the potato. Repeat these cuts every 5 mm/¼ inch along the length of the potato. Carefully ease 2–4 of the slices apart and slip in a few rosemary sprigs. Repeat with remaining potatoes. Brush with the oil and season well with salt and pepper.

2 Place the seasoned potatoes in a large roasting tin. Add the parsnips, carrots and leeks to the potatoes in the tin, cover with a wire rack or trivet.

3 Beat the butter and lemon rind together and season to taste. Smear the chicken with the lemon butter and place on the rack over the vegetables.

4 Roast in the preheated oven for 1 hour 40 minutes, basting the chicken and vegetables occasionally, until cooked thoroughly. The juices should run clear when the thigh is pierced with a skewer. Place the cooked chicken on a warmed serving platter, arrange the roast vegetables around it and serve immediately.

FOOD FACT

Hasselback potatoes were named after the Stockholm restaurant of the same name. Using chopsticks is a great way of ensuring that you slice just far enough through the potatoes so that they fan out during cooking. The potatoes can be given an attractive golden finish by mixing ¼ tsp ground turmeric or paprika with the oil.

FRAGRANT FRUIT PILAF

INGREDIENTS   Serves 4–6

50 g/2 oz butter
6 green cardamom pods
1 cinnamon stick
2 bay leaves
450 g/1 lb basmati rice
600 ml/1 pint chicken stock
1 onion, peeled and finely
  chopped
50 g/2 oz flaked almonds
50 g/2 oz shelled pistachios,
  roughly chopped

125 g/4 oz ready-to-eat dried
  figs, roughly chopped
50 g/2 oz ready-to-eat dried
  apricots, roughly chopped
275 g/10 oz skinless chicken
  breast fillets, cut into chunks
salt and freshly ground black
  pepper
fresh parsley or coriander
  leaves, to garnish

1 Melt half the butter in a saucepan or casserole dish with a tight-fitting lid. Add the cardamom pods and cinnamon stick and cook for about 30 seconds before adding the bay leaves and rice. Stir well to coat the rice in the butter and add the stock. Bring to the boil, cover tightly and cook very gently for 15 minutes. Remove from the heat and leave to stand for a further 5 minutes.

2 Melt the remaining butter in a wok and when foaming, add the onion, flaked almonds and pistachios. Stir-fry for 3–4 minutes until the nuts are beginning to brown. Remove and reserve.

3 Reduce the heat slightly and add the dried figs, apricots and chicken and continue stir-frying for a further 7–8 minutes until the chicken is cooked through. Return the nuts mixture and toss to mix.

4 Remove from the heat, then remove the cinnamon stick and bay leaves. Add the cooked rice and stir together well to mix. Season to taste with salt and pepper. Garnish with parsley or coriander leaves and serve immediately.

TASTY TIP

Leave the chicken out of this recipe, reducing the cooking time accordingly, to make a tasty side dish or vegetarian option.

LEG OF LAMB WITH MINTED RICE

INGREDIENTS   Serves 4

1 tbsp olive oil

1 medium onion, peeled and finely chopped

1 garlic clove, peeled and crushed

1 celery stalk, trimmed and chopped

1 large mild red chilli, deseeded and chopped

75 g/3 oz long-grain rice

150 ml/¼ pint lamb or chicken stock

2 tbsp freshly chopped mint

salt and freshly ground black pepper

1.4 kg/3 lb boned leg of lamb

freshly cooked vegetables, to serve

1 Preheat the oven to 190°C/ 375°F/Gas Mark 5, 10 minutes before roasting. Heat the oil in a frying pan and gently cook the onion for 5 minutes. Stir in the garlic, celery and chilli and continue to cook for 3–4 minutes.

2 Place the rice and the stock in a large saucepan and cook, covered, for 10–12 minutes or until the rice is tender and all the liquid is absorbed. Stir in the onion and celery mixture, then leave to cool. Once the rice mixture is cold, stir in the chopped mint and season to taste with salt and pepper.

3 Place the boned lamb skin-side down and spoon the rice mixture along the centre of the meat. Roll up the meat to enclose the stuffing and tie securely with string. Place in a roasting tin and roast in the preheated oven for

1 hour 20 minutes, or until cooked to personal preference. Remove from the oven and leave to rest in a warm place for 20 minutes, before carving. Serve with a selection of cooked vegetables.

HELPFUL HINT

Weigh the lamb after stuffing and allow it to come to room temperature before roasting. For medium-cooked lamb, allow 25 minutes per 450 g/ 1 lb plus 25 minutes; for well-done, allow 30 minutes per 450 g/1 lb plus 30 minutes. Use a meat thermometer to check whether the joint is cooked, or push a fine skewer into the thickest part: for rare meat the juices will be slightly red, for medium they will be pink and when well-done, the juices will run clear.

CROWN ROAST OF LAMB

INGREDIENTS   Serves 6

1 lamb crown roast
salt and freshly ground black
 pepper
1 tbsp sunflower oil
1 small onion, peeled and
 finely chopped
2–3 garlic cloves, peeled and
 crushed
2 celery stalks, trimmed and
 finely chopped
125 g/4 oz cooked mixed
 basmati and wild rice

75 g/3 oz ready-to-eat-dried
 apricots, chopped
50 g/2 oz pine nuts, toasted
1 tbsp finely grated orange
 rind
2 tbsp freshly chopped
 coriander
1 small egg, beaten
freshly roasted potatoes and
 green vegetables, to serve

1 Preheat the oven to 180°C/ 350°F/Gas Mark 4, about 10 minutes before roasting. Wipe the crown roast and season the cavity with salt and pepper. Place in a roasting tin and cover the ends of the bones with small pieces of tinfoil.

2 Heat the oil in a small saucepan and cook the onion, garlic and celery for 5 minutes, then remove the saucepan from the heat. Add the cooked rice with the apricots, pine nuts, orange rind and coriander. Season with salt and pepper, then stir in the egg and mix well.

3 Carefully spoon the prepared stuffing into the cavity of the lamb, then roast in the preheated oven for 1–1½ hours. Remove the lamb from the oven and remove and discard the tinfoil from the

bones. Return to the oven and continue to cook for a further 15 minutes, or until cooked to personal preference.

4 Remove from the oven and leave to rest for 10 minutes before serving with the roast potatoes and freshly cooked vegetables.

FOOD FACT

Best end of neck consists of 6–7 small chops. Crown roast is made by joining 2 best ends together, making a perfect central cavity to fill with stuffing. When ready to serve, the trimmed cutlet bones may be topped, if liked, with paper frills, looking like tiny chefs' hats.

SWEET-&-SOUR SHREDDED BEEF

INGREDIENTS   Serves 4

350 g/12 oz rump steak
1 tsp sesame oil
2 tbsp Chinese rice wine or
   sweet sherry
2 tbsp dark soy sauce
1 tsp cornflour
4 tbsp pineapple juice
2 tsp soft light brown sugar
1 tsp sherry vinegar
salt and freshly ground black
   pepper
2 tbsp groundnut oil

2 medium carrots, peeled and
   cut into matchsticks
125 g/4 oz mangetout peas,
   trimmed and cut into
   matchsticks
1 bunch spring onions,
   trimmed and shredded
2 garlic cloves, peeled and
   crushed
1 tbsp toasted sesame seeds
freshly cooked Thai fragrant
   rice, to serve

1 Cut the steak across the grain into thin strips. Put in a bowl with the sesame oil, 1 tablespoon of the Chinese rice wine or sherry and 1 tablespoon of the soy sauce. Mix well, cover and leave to marinate in the refrigerator for 30 minutes.

2 In a small bowl, blend together the cornflour with the remaining Chinese rice wine or sherry, then stir in the pineapple juice, remaining soy sauce, sugar and vinegar. Season with a little salt and pepper and reserve.

3 Heat a wok until hot, add 1 tablespoon of the oil, then drain the beef, reserving the marinade, and stir-fry for 1–2 minutes, or until browned. Remove from the wok and reserve.

4 Add the remaining oil to the wok then add the carrots and stir-fry for 1 minute, then add the mangetout peas and spring onions and stir-fry for a further 1 minute.

5 Return the beef to the wok with the sauce, reserved marinade and garlic. Continue cooking for 1 minute or until the vegetables are tender and the sauce is bubbling. Turn the stir-fry into a warmed serving dish, sprinkle with toasted sesame seeds and serve immediately with the Thai fragrant rice.

HELPFUL HINT

It is important to slice the beef across the grain so that it will hold together when it is being cooked.

PORK WITH TOFU

INGREDIENTS — Serves 4

450 g/1 lb smoked firm tofu, drained
2 tbsp groundnut oil
3 garlic cloves, peeled and crushed
2.5 cm/1 inch piece fresh root ginger, peeled and finely chopped
350 g/12 oz fresh pork mince
1 tbsp chilli powder

1 tsp sugar
2 tbsp Chinese rice wine
1 tbsp dark soy sauce
1 tbsp light soy sauce
2 tbsp yellow bean sauce
1 tsp Szechuan peppercorns
75 ml/3 fl oz chicken stock
spring onions, trimmed and finely sliced, to garnish
fried rice, to serve

1 Cut the tofu into 1 cm/½ inch cubes and place in a sieve to drain. Place the tofu on absorbent kitchen paper to dry thoroughly for another 10 minutes.

2 Heat the wok, add the groundnut oil and when hot, add the garlic and ginger. Stir-fry for a few seconds to flavour the oil, but not to colour the vegetables. Add the pork mince and stir-fry for 3 minutes, or until the pork is sealed and there are no lumps in the mince.

3 Add all the remaining ingredients except for the tofu. Bring the mixture to the boil, then reduce the heat to low. Add the tofu and mix it in gently, taking care not to break up the tofu chunks, but ensuring an even mixture of ingredients. Simmer, uncovered, for 15 minutes, or until the tofu is tender. Turn into a warmed serving dish, garnish with sliced spring onions and serve immediately with fried rice.

HELPFUL HINT

When adding spices such as garlic and ginger to hot oil, make sure you only cook them for a few seconds to develop their flavour, moving them around the pan all the time, and do not allow them to burn or they will taste bitter. When adding the pork mince, break down the lumps of meat as much as possible, so the mince is really fine.

OSSOBUCO WITH SAFFRON RISOTTO

INGREDIENTS — Serves 4

125 g/4 oz butter
2 tbsp olive oil
4 large pieces of shin of veal (often sold as ossobuco)
2 onions, peeled and roughly chopped
2 garlic cloves, peeled and finely chopped
300 ml/½ pint white wine
5 plum tomatoes, peeled and chopped

1 tbsp tomato purée
salt and freshly ground black pepper
2 tbsp freshly chopped parsley
grated rind of 1 small lemon
few strands of saffron, crushed
350 g/12 oz Arborio rice
1.3 litres/2¼ pints chicken stock, heated
50 g/2 oz Parmesan cheese, grated

1 Heat 50 g/2 oz butter with half the oil in a large saucepan and add the pieces of veal. Brown lightly on both sides, then transfer to a plate. Add half the onion and garlic and cook gently for about 10 minutes until the onion is just golden.

2 Return the veal to the saucepan along with the white wine, tomatoes and tomato purée. Season lightly with salt and pepper, cover and bring to a gentle simmer. Cook very gently for 1 hour. Uncover and cook for a further 30 minutes until the meat is cooked and the sauce is reduced and thickened. Season to taste. Mix together the remaining garlic, parsley and lemon rind and reserve.

3 Meanwhile, slowly melt the remaining butter and oil in a large deep-sided frying pan. Add the remaining onion and cook gently for 5–7 minutes until just brown. Add the saffron and stir for a few seconds, then add the rice. Cook for a further minute until the rice is well coated in oil and butter.

5 Begin adding the stock a ladleful at a time, stirring well after each addition of stock and waiting until it is absorbed before adding the next. Continue in this way until all the stock is used. Remove from the heat and stir in the grated Parmesan cheese and seasoning.

6 Spoon a little of the saffron risotto onto each of 4 serving plates. Top with the ossobuco and sauce and sprinkle over the reserved garlic and parsley mixture. Serve immediately.

PORK LOIN STUFFED WITH ORANGE & HAZELNUT RICE

INGREDIENTS
Serves 4

15 g/½ oz butter

1 shallot, peeled and finely chopped

50 g/2 oz long-grain brown rice

175 ml/6 fl oz vegetable stock

½ orange

25 g/1 oz ready-to-eat dried prunes, stoned and chopped

25 g/1 oz hazelnuts, roasted and roughly chopped

1 small egg, beaten

1 tbsp freshly chopped parsley

salt and freshly ground pepper

450 g/1 lb boneless pork tenderloin or fillet, trimmed

FOR THE RICE:

steamed courgettes

carrots

1 Preheat the oven to 190°C/ 375°F/Gas Mark 5, 10 minutes before required. Heat the butter in a small saucepan, add the shallot and cook gently for 2–3 minutes until softened. Add the rice and stir well for 1 minute. Add the stock, stir well and bring to the boil. Cover tightly and simmer gently for 30 minutes until the rice is tender and all the liquid is absorbed. Leave to cool.

2 Grate the orange rind and reserve. Remove the white pith and chop the orange flesh finely. Mix together the orange rind and flesh, prunes, hazelnuts, cooled rice, egg and parsley. Season to taste with salt and pepper.

3 Cut the fillet in half, then using a sharp knife, split the pork fillet lengthways almost in two, forming a pocket, leaving it just attached. Open out the pork and put between 2 pieces of clingfilm. Flatten using a meat mallet until about half its original thickness. Spoon the filling into the pocket and close the fillet over. Tie along the length with kitchen string at regular intervals.

4 Put the pork fillet in a small roasting tray and cook in the top of the preheated oven for 25–30 minutes, or until the meat is just tender. Remove from the oven and allow to rest for 5 minutes. Slice into rounds and serve with steamed courgettes and carrots.

TASTY TIP

For an alternative stuffing try adding pine nuts and thyme.

BROWN RICE SPICED PILAF

INGREDIENTS   Serves 4

1 tbsp vegetable oil

1 tbsp blanched almonds, flaked or chopped

1 onion, peeled and chopped

1 carrot, peeled and diced

225 g/8 oz flat mushrooms, sliced thickly

¼ tsp cinnamon

large pinch dried chilli flakes

50 g/2 oz dried apricots, roughly chopped

25 g/1 oz currants

zest of 1 orange

350 g/12 oz brown basmati rice

900 ml/1½ pints vegetable stock

2 tbsp freshly chopped coriander

2 tbsp freshly snipped chives

salt and freshly ground black pepper

snipped chives, to garnish

1 Preheat the oven to 200°C/ 400°F/Gas Mark 6. Heat the oil in a large flameproof casserole and add the almonds. Cook for 1–2 minutes until just browning. (Be very careful as the nuts will burn very easily).

2 Add the onion and carrot. Cook for 5 minutes until softened and starting to turn brown. Add the mushrooms and cook for a further 5 minutes, stirring often.

3 Add the cinnamon and chilli flakes and cook for about 30 seconds before adding the apricots, currants, orange zest and rice.

4 Stir together well and add the stock. Bring to the boil, cover tightly and transfer to the preheated oven. Cook for 45 minutes until the rice and vegetables are tender.

5 Stir the coriander and chives into the pilaf and season to taste with salt and pepper. Garnish with the extra chives and serve immediately.

FOOD FACT

The less processed or refined foods are the higher the content of nutrient. Brown basmati rice, in particular, is one of the best rices to eat, releasing carbohydrate slowly into the blood thereby maintaining the body's energy levels as well as supplying the body with fibre.

THAI NOODLES & VEGETABLES WITH TOFU

INGREDIENTS   Serves 4

225 g/8 oz firm tofu

2 tbsp soy sauce

rind of 1 lime, grated

2 lemon grass stalks

1 red chilli

1 litre/1¾ pint
vegetable stock

2 slices fresh root
ginger, peeled

2 garlic cloves, peeled

2 sprigs of fresh coriander

175 g/6 oz dried thread
egg noodles

125 g/4 oz shiitake or button
mushrooms, sliced if large

2 carrots, peeled and
cut into matchsticks

125 g/4 oz mangetout

125 g/4 oz bok choy or
other Chinese leaf

1 tbsp freshly
chopped coriander

salt and freshly ground
black pepper

coriander sprigs, to garnish

1 Drain the tofu well and cut into cubes. Put into a shallow dish with the soy sauce and lime rind. Stir well to coat and leave to marinate for 30 minutes.

2 Meanwhile, put the lemon grass and chilli on a chopping board and bruise with the side of a large knife, ensuring the blade is pointing away from you. Put the vegetable stock in a large saucepan and add the lemon grass, chilli, ginger, garlic, and coriander. Bring to the boil, cover and simmer gently for 20 minutes.

3 Strain the stock into a clean pan. Return to the boil and add the noodles, tofu and its marinade and the mushrooms. Simmer gently for 4 minutes.

4 Add the carrots, mangetout, bok choy, coriander and simmer for a further 3–4 minutes until the vegetables are just tender. Season to taste with salt and pepper. Garnish with coriander sprigs. Serve immediately.

FOOD FACT

Tofu is a curd derived from soya and is an extremely protein-rich food that is virtually-fat free. Recent studies suggest that there are many health benefits to incorporating soya into your diet not least for its cancer-prevention properties.

PAD THAI NOODLES WITH USHROOMS

INGREDIENTS   Serves 4

125 g/4 oz flat rice noodles
  or rice vermicelli
1 tbsp vegetable oil
2 garlic cloves, peeled
  and finely chopped
1 medium egg, lightly beaten
225 g/8 oz mixed
  mushrooms, including
  shiitake, oyster, field, brown
  and wild mushrooms
2 tbsp lemon juice

1½ tbsp Thai fish sauce
½ tsp sugar
½ tsp cayenne pepper
2 spring onions, trimmed and
  cut into 2.5 cm/1 inch pieces
50 g/2 oz fresh beansprouts

TO GARNISH:
chopped roasted peanuts
freshly chopped coriander

1 Cook the noodles according to the packet instructions. Drain well and reserve.

2 Heat a wok or large frying pan. Add the oil and garlic. Fry until just golden. Add the egg and stir quickly to break it up.

3 Cook for a few seconds before adding the noodles and mushrooms. Scrape down the sides of the pan to ensure they mix with the egg and garlic.

4 Add the lemon juice, fish sauce, sugar, cayenne pepper, spring onions and half of the beansprouts, stirring quickly all the time.

5 Cook over a high heat for a further 2–3 minutes until everything is heated through.

6 Turn on to a serving plate. Top with the remaining beansprouts. Garnish with the chopped peanuts and coriander and serve immediately.

TASTY TIP

Far Eastern cooking is by its nature low fat and is often based around its fragrant spices. An aromatic alternative to this dish is to replace the lemon used in this dish with lemon grass. Discard the outer leaves, finely chop and add with the other ingredients in step 4.

WARM POTATO, PEAR & PECAN SALAD

INGREDIENTS Serves 4

900 g/2 lb new potatoes,
  preferably red-skinned,
  unpeeled
salt and freshly ground black
  pepper
1 tsp Dijon mustard
2 tsp white wine vinegar

3 tbsp groundnut oil
1 tbsp hazelnut or walnut oil
2 tsp poppy seeds
2 firm ripe dessert pears
2 tsp lemon juice
175 g/6 oz baby spinach leaves
75 g/3 oz toasted pecan nuts

1 Scrub the potatoes, then cook in a saucepan of lightly salted boiling water for 15 minutes, or until tender. Drain, cut into halves, or quarters if large, and place in a serving bowl.

2 In a small bowl or jug, whisk together the mustard and vinegar. Gradually add the oils until the mixture begins to thicken. Stir in the poppy seeds and season to taste with salt and pepper.

3 Pour about two-thirds of the dressing over the hot potatoes and toss gently to coat. Leave until the potatoes have soaked up the dressing and are just warm.

4 Meanwhile, quarter and core the pears. Cut into thin slices, then sprinkle with the lemon juice to prevent them from going brown. Add to the potatoes with the spinach leaves and toasted pecan nuts. Gently mix together.

5 Drizzle the remaining dressing over the salad. Serve immediately before the spinach starts to wilt.

HANDY HINT

To toast the pecan nuts, place on a baking tray in a single layer and cook in a preheated oven at 180°C/350°F/Gas Mark 4 for 5 minutes, or under a medium grill for 3–4 minutes, turning frequently. Watch them carefully – they burn easily. If you can not get red-skinned new potatoes for this dish, add colour by using red-skinned pears instead. Look out for *Red Bartlett*, *Red Williams* and *Napolian*.

WILD RICE & BACON SALAD WITH SMOKED CHICKEN

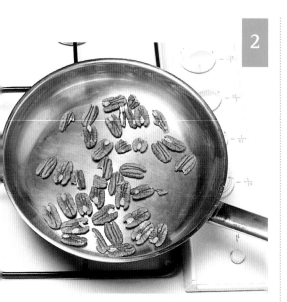

INGREDIENTS   Serves 4

150 g/5 oz wild rice
50 g/2 oz pecan or walnut
   halves
1 tbsp vegetable oil
4 slices smoked bacon, diced
3–4 shallots, peeled and finely
   chopped
75 ml/3 fl oz walnut oil

2–3 tbsp sherry or cider
   vinegar
2 tbsp freshly chopped dill
salt and freshly ground black
   pepper
275 g/10 oz smoked chicken or
   duck breast, thinly sliced
dill sprigs, to garnish

1 Put the wild rice in a medium saucepan with 600 ml/1 pint water and bring to the boil, stirring once or twice. Reduce the heat, cover and simmer gently for 30–50 minutes, depending on the texture you prefer, chewy or tender. Using a fork, gently fluff into a large bowl and leave to cool slightly.

2 Meanwhile, toast the nuts in a frying pan over a medium heat for 2 minutes, or until they are fragrant and lightly coloured, stirring and tossing frequently. Cool, then chop coarsely and add to the rice.

3 Heat the oil in the frying pan over a medium heat. Add the bacon and cook, stirring from time to time, for 3–4 minutes, or until crisp and brown. Remove from the pan and drain on absorbent kitchen paper. Add the shallots to the pan and cook for 4 minutes, or until just softened, stirring

from time to time. Stir into the rice and nuts, with the drained bacon pieces.

4 Whisk the walnut oil, vinegar, half the dill and salt and pepper in a small bowl until combined. Pour the dressing over the rice mixture and toss well to combine. Mix the chicken and the remaining chopped dill into the rice, then spoon into bowls and garnish each serving with a dill sprig. Serve slightly warm, or at room temperature.

FOOD FACT

Both smoked chicken and duck have a delicate smoky flavour which comes from being first cold-smoked, then briefly hot-smoked. You can, of course, use plain roasted chicken or duck if you prefer.

MEDITERRANEAN POTATO SALAD

INGREDIENTS   Serves 4

700 g/1½ lb small waxy
potatoes

2 red onions, peeled and
roughly chopped

1 yellow pepper, deseeded
and roughly chopped

1 green pepper, deseeded and
roughly chopped

6 tbsp extra-virgin olive oil

125 g/4 oz ripe tomatoes,
chopped

50 g/2 oz pitted black olives,
sliced

125 g/4 oz feta cheese

3 tbsp freshly chopped
parsley

2 tbsp white wine vinegar

1 tsp Dijon mustard

1 tsp clear honey

salt and freshly ground black
pepper

sprigs of fresh parsley,
to garnish

1 Preheat the oven to 200°C/
400°F/Gas Mark 6. Place the
potatoes in a large saucepan of
salted water, bring to the boil and
simmer until just tender. Do not
overcook. Drain and plunge into
cold water, to stop them from
cooking further.

2 Place the onions in a bowl
with the yellow and green
peppers, then pour over 2
tablespoons of the olive oil. Stir
and spoon onto a large baking
tray. Cook in the preheated oven
for 25–30 minutes, or until the
vegetables are tender and lightly
charred in places, stirring
occasionally. Remove from the
oven and transfer to a large bowl.

3 Cut the potatoes into bite-
sized pieces and mix with the
roasted onions and peppers. Add
the tomatoes and olives to the
potatoes. Crumble over the feta

cheese and sprinkle with
the chopped parsley.

4 Whisk together the remaining
olive oil, vinegar, mustard
and honey, then season to taste
with salt and pepper. Pour the
dressing over the potatoes and
toss gently together. Garnish
with parsley sprigs and serve
immediately.

FOOD FACT

Tomatoes are such an integral
part of many cuisines, that it
is hard to believe they were
only introduced to Europe
from the Americas a few
hundred years ago. There are
lots of new flavoursome
varieties now available to try.
Those sold still attached to
the vine tend to have a
particularly good flavour.

INDEX